EP Language Arts 7
Workbook

This book belongs to:

_____

EP Language Arts 7 Workbook

This workbook, made by Tina Rutherford with permission from Easy Peasy All-in-One Homeschool, is based on the language arts component of Easy Peasy's curriculum. For EP's online curriculum visit allinonehomeschool.com

Cover design by Yuletide Media: www.yuletidemedia.com

ISBN: 9781792612336

First Edition: April, 2019

About this Workbook

This is an offline workbook for Easy Peasy All-in-One Homeschool's Language Arts 7 course. We've modified and expanded upon the online activities and printable worksheets available at the Easy Peasy All-in-One Homeschool website (www.allinonehomeschool.com) so that your child can work offline if desired. Whether you use the online or offline versions, or a combination of both, your child will enjoy these supplements to the Easy Peasy Language Arts course.

How to use this Workbook

This workbook is designed to be used in conjunction with Easy Peasy's Language Arts 7 Lesson Guide. As you and your child proceed through the Lesson Guide, use this workbook to exercise your child's language arts skills.

This workbook follows the EP online Language Arts course in sequential order, providing activity worksheets which can replace online activities and printable worksheets. However, this workbook does not include activity worksheets for the longer writing assignments. As such, this book does not contain 180 days of worksheets. The Lesson Guide will contain all writing assignments to make the course complete. There is also a brief description of them on the completion chart pages that follow (grayed out boxes denote no worksheet). If possible, allow your child to do these writing assignments on the computer to get practice typing and formatting papers.

The activity worksheets are designed with the following guidelines in mind:

- **To supplement daily lessons**
  This workbook on its own supplements, but does not replace, EP's daily lessons. Be sure to check the daily lesson on the website or in the Lesson Guide before having your child do the workbook activities.

- **To serve as an alternative to online activities**
  This workbook serves as an alternative to the activities posted online, providing offline activities in sufficient quantities and varieties to challenge your child. When used in conjunction with the Lesson Guide, this workbook becomes a complete offline course.

Please note, in the various places where nouns, verbs, adjectives, and adverbs are practiced, certain words can be categorized in more than one place (you can go for a swim [noun] or you can swim [verb]). If your child marks one of them differently than the answer key indicates, have a conversation with them to find out why.

- The solutions are on the website as well as in the Lesson Guide and are **not included** in this workbook.

Completion Chart for Lessons 1 - 45

①	writing - motto	⑯	spelling	㉛	writing
②	writing - poem	⑰	spelling - hangman	㉜	proofreading
③	writing - poem	⑱	spelling - unscramble	㉝	proofreading
④	writing - psalm	⑲	spelling	㉞	writing - friendly letter
⑤	writing - poem	⑳	spelling	㉟	proofreading/parts of speech
⑥	spelling	㉑	spelling - crossword	㊱	essay - organization
⑦	spelling - hangman	㉒	proofreading	㊲	essay
⑧	spelling - unscramble	㉓	proofreading	㊳	essay
⑨	spelling	㉔	proofreading	㊴	essay
⑩	spelling	㉕	writing	㊵	editing
⑪	spelling	㉖	proofreading	㊶	writing - t-shirt design
⑫	spelling - hangman	㉗	proofreading	㊷	writing - book review
⑬	spelling - unscramble	㉘	writing	㊸	parts of speech/ book review
⑭	spelling	㉙	proofreading	㊹	parts of speech/ book review
⑮	spelling	㉚	proofreading	㊺	book review

*Grayed out boxes denote writing assignments that don't have a corresponding worksheet in this book.
Full writing assignments can be found online or in the Parent's Guide*

Completion Chart for Lessons 46 - 90

(46)	possessives/plurals	(61)	writing	(76)	spelling/descriptive essay
(47)	proofreading	(62)	writing - personal response	(77)	proofreading/ descriptive essay
(48)	writing - summary	(63)	writing - personal response	(78)	proofreading/ descriptive essay
(49)	proofreading	(64)	writing - personal response	(79)	proofreading/ descriptive essay
(50)	writing	(65)	editing - personal response	(80)	descriptive essay
(51)	spelling - unscramble	(66)	spelling - crossword	(81)	descriptive essay
(52)	parts of speech	(67)	punctuation/ capitalization	(82)	descriptive essay
(53)	spelling - word search	(68)	participle phrases	(83)	descriptive essay
(54)	gerunds	(69)	participles/gerunds	(84)	descriptive essay
(55)	writing - 15 minutes	(70)	writing - short story	(85)	editing
(56)	idiom hangman	(71)	nouns	(86)	spelling/compare and contrast essay
(57)	spelling - word search	(72)	descriptive essay	(87)	grammar/compare and contrast essay
(58)	gerunds	(73)	similes/metaphors	(88)	compare and contrast essay
(59)	gerunds	(74)	descriptive paragraph	(89)	nouns/compare and contrast essay
(60)	writing - 15 minutes	(75)	descriptive essay	(90)	plurals/compare and contrast essay

Completion Chart for Lessons 91-135

(91)	compare and contrast essay	(106)	spelling	(121)	spelling
(92)	paragraphs/essay	(107)	apostrophes/writing - log entry	(122)	spelling - hangman
(93)	paragraphs/essay	(108)	lose vs. loose/ writing - log entry	(123)	spelling - unscramble
(94)	pronouns/editing	(109)	who vs. whom/ writing - log entry	(124)	spelling
(95)	pronouns/editing	(110)	writing - log entry	(125)	spelling
(96)	grammar review	(111)	proofreading	(126)	spelling
(97)	pronouns/writing organization	(112)	plurals and possessives	(127)	spelling - hangman
(98)	pronouns/writing voice	(113)	writing - 10 minutes	(128)	spelling - unscramble
(99)	pronouns/word choice	(114)	plurals and possessives	(129)	spelling
(100)	pronouns/sentences	(115)	writing - 10 minutes	(130)	spelling
(101)	writing - book report	(116)	possessives	(131)	inifinitives
(102)	writing - book report	(117)	writing - point of view story	(132)	spelling- word search
(103)	plurals	(118)	writing - point of view story	(133)	spelling
(104)	plurals and possessives	(119)	writing - point of view story	(34)	gerunds/infinitives
(105)	possessives	(120)	writing - point of view story	(135)	writing - song

Completion Chart for Lessons 136-180

(136)	writing - sentence types	(151)	spelling	(166)	anthropomorphism
(137)	dangling modifiers	(152)	metaphors/genre	(167)	lie vs. lay
(138)	dangling modifiers	(153)	sentence structure/ characters	(168)	writing - novel
(139)	dangling modifiers	(154)	conflict	(169)	writing - novel
(140)	writing	(155)	sidekicks/ descriptive writing	(170)	writing - novel
(141)	spelling	(156)	setting/sentence types	(171)	personification
(142)	reading comprehension	(157)	minor setting/ parallel sentences	(172)	writing - novel
(143)	reading comprehension	(158)	complications	(173)	writing - novel
(144)	reading comprehension	(159)	plot chart	(174)	writing - novel
(145)	reading comprehension	(160)	chapter list	(175)	writing - novel
(146)	reading comprehension	(161)	irony/oxymorons	(176)	writing - novel
(147)	reading comprehension	(162)	writing - novel	(177)	alliteration
(148)	reading comprehension	(163)	dialogue	(178)	onomatopoeia
(149)	reading comprehension	(164)	uncommon punctuation	(179)	writing - novel
(150)	reading comprehension	(165)	metaphor	(180)	writing - novel

Lesson 1: Writing

Write a motto or catchphrase for the school year using at least one of the words from the box. (NOTE: *the teaching lesson for this and every worksheet is located in the Lesson Guide. That separate book is necessary to make the course complete.*)

Conflate: to blend together

Denouement: conclusion; ending

Elixir: a good potion

Epiphany: a sudden revelation

Evanescent: fleeting; brief; temporary

Leisure: free time

Plethora: overabundance

Quintessential: typical; standard

Tintinnabulation: tinkling

Vestigial: in small amounts

Wherewithal: means or ability

_____

_____

_____

_____

_____

Write a poem with the same rhythm and rhyme scheme as the poem *Hope is the Thing With Feathers* by Emily Dickinson.

> *"Hope" is the thing with feathers*
> *That perches in the soul*
> *And sings the tune without the words*
> *And never stops at all,*
>
> *And sweetest in the gale is heard;*
> *And sore must be the storm*
> *That could abash the little bird*
> *That kept so many warm.*
>
> *I've heard it in the chillest land*
> *And on the strangest sea,*
> *Yet never, in extremity,*
> *It asked a crumb of me.*

_____

_____

_____

_____

_____

_____

_____

Write a poem with the same rhythm and rhyme scheme as the poem *A Thanksgiving to God, for his House* by Robert Herrick.

> *Lord, Thou hast given me a cell*
> *Wherein to dwell,*
> *A little house, whose humble roof*
> *Is weather-proof:*
> *Under the spars of which I lie*
> *Both soft, and dry;*
> *Where Thou my chamber for to ward*
> *Hast set a guard*
> *Of harmless thoughts, to watch and keep*
> *Me, while I sleep.*

_____

_____

_____

_____

_____

_____

_____

Lesson 4: Writing

Write a psalm that uses as least one simile.

_____

_____

_____

_____

_____

_____

_____

_____

_____

Need some help? If you're having trouble coming up with a simile, maybe one of these can spark some creativity: God is like... we are like... our sins are as... His love is as...

Tell a story using at least two couplets.

_____

_____

_____

_____

_____

_____

_____

_____

_____

_____

> *Frozen North, and chilling East,*
> *Sounded tempests to the feast*
> *Of the forest's whispering fleeces,*
> *Since men knew nor rent nor leases.*
>
> -John Keats

Lesson 6: Spelling

See how many words you can spell correctly the first time as they are read to you from the Lesson Guide. Learn from any mistakes you make.

_____   _____

_____   _____

_____   _____

_____   _____

_____   _____

_____   _____

_____   _____

_____   _____

Lesson 7: Spelling - Unscramble

Unscramble your spelling words.

EIRAIBVAOTBN _____

AEULDTSBAJ _____

OABRBS _____

SOOTASIICNA _____

BCSLICEESA _____

CEAANDENTT _____

TAVNIEHECEM _____

TNTMIACDEA _____

ALLBOUYSET _____

RSCAE _____

YZANELA _____

HAFGNA _____

SASNLYAI _____

HAIURTOTY _____

CLIIARATIF _____

DVESAI _____

NCSIAAESST _____

VCDEIA _____

Lesson 8: Spelling

Fill in the blanks with the correct spelling word. Be sure to spell it correctly!

The park included three _____ of luscious grass.

The seatbelt was _____ to fit her small waist.

I would _____ against speaking disrespectfully.

The _____ kept her warm when the heat went out.

What's your _____ of this situation?

This _____ sweetener has an aftertaste.

Are you _____ certain you turned off the stove?

What has been your greatest _____ this year?

The sign said, "No _____."

Can you offer your _____ to that lady?

What's the postal _____ for Massachusetts?

Do you submit to those in _____?

Her _____ at the meetings was sporadic at best.

The sponge will _____ the entire spill.

What's your _____ on this topic?

The playground was _____ to all kids.

When I _____ the budget, I see a deficit.

I have a close _____ with my co-worker.

Play hangman! See if you can figure out your spelling words in ten guesses or less. Cross out letters you've guessed to help yourself keep track. The words are in the Lesson Guide.

A B C D E F G H I J K L M N O P Q R S T U V W X Y Z

__ __ __ __ __ __ __ __ __ __

A B C D E F G H I J K L M N O P Q R S T U V W X Y Z

__ __ __ __ __ __

A B C D E F G H I J K L M N O P Q R S T U V W X Y Z

__ __ __ __ __ __ __

A B C D E F G H I J K L M N O P Q R S T U V W X Y Z

__ __ __ __ __ __ __

A B C D E F G H I J K L M N O P Q R S T U V W X Y Z

__ __ __ __ __ __ __ __

A B C D E F G H I J K L M N O P Q R S T U V W X Y Z

__ __ __ __ __ __ __ __ __

Lesson 10: Spelling

See how many words you can spell correctly now as they are read to you. Learn from any mistakes you make.

_____   _____

_____   _____

_____   _____

_____   _____

_____   _____

_____   _____

_____   _____

_____   _____

Lesson 11: Spelling

See how many words you can spell correctly the first time as they are read to you from the Lesson Guide. Learn from any mistakes you make.

_____   _____

_____   _____

_____   _____

_____   _____

_____   _____

_____   _____

_____   _____

Lesson 12: Spelling - Unscramble

Unscramble your spelling words.

TBUEOQU   _____

ETRACAIB   _____

PTAALIC   _____

ALGEB   _____

UEBRUA   _____

CEYLICB   _____

ANINMONC   _____

DBUOVEARL   _____

PMGNIACA   _____

NODBRUAY   _____

TNOECFTI   _____

ICPOLTA   _____

EIMINCTTOPO   _____

TILUCPR   _____

SIBTCUI   _____

NMOITMCOO   _____

NAOALGCIONUTSTR   _____

RBAIREZ   _____

Lesson 13: Spelling

Fill in the blanks with the correct spelling word. Be sure to spell it correctly!

Iris picked a lovely _____ of wildflowers.

_____ are in order for the winners.

The state _____ building is located downtown.

The infection in my throat was caused by _____.

Do you put _____ on your applesauce?

The presidential _____ was successful.

I rode my _____ to work yesterday.

The _____ comment left me scratching my head.

What's all the _____ outside?

The bushes form a natural _____ for the property.

Do you like cream cheese on your _____?

The _____ winds its way by the beautiful park.

The crowd threw _____ as the newlyweds ran past.

The _____ of California is Sacramento.

Chase likes to put honey on his morning _____.

Sara put her jewelry box on top of the _____.

It seems a mouse was the cookie thief _____.

The _____ was fierce at the spelling bee.

Lesson 14: Spelling - Hangman

Play hangman! See if you can figure out your spelling words in ten guesses or less. Cross out letters you've guessed to help yourself keep track. The words are in the Lesson Guide.

A B C D E F G H I J K L M N O P Q R S T U V W X Y Z

— — — — — — — — —

A B C D E F G H I J K L M N O P Q R S T U V W X Y Z

— — — — — — — — —

A B C D E F G H I J K L M N O P Q R S T U V W X Y Z

— — — — — — — —

A B C D E F G H I J K L M N O P Q R S T U V W X Y Z

— — — — — — — — —

A B C D E F G H I J K L M N O P Q R S T U V W X Y Z

— — — — — — — — —

A B C D E F G H I J K L M N O P Q R S T U V W X Y Z

— — — — — — — — —

Lesson 15: Spelling

See how many words you can spell correctly now as they are read to you. Learn from any mistakes you make.

_____   _____

_____   _____

_____   _____

_____   _____

_____   _____

_____   _____

_____   _____

_____   _____

Lesson 16: Spelling

See how many words you can spell correctly the first time as they are read to you from the Lesson Guide. Learn from any mistakes you make.

_____   _____

_____   _____

_____   _____

_____   _____

_____   _____

_____   _____

_____   _____

_____   _____

Lesson 17: Spelling - Unscramble

Unscramble your spelling words.

TDEDOONRA _____

IENTEDV _____

EIHSMEAPZ _____

AISSISDML _____

EEICDEV _____

MRSERBAAS _____

YRMEETELX _____

YDDLEAE _____

XIETIBH _____

NRCECLIE _____

ENAROXADRYRTI _____

EIAMTDRE _____

OREACCYDM _____

XHUIEINSGT _____

CNTEXTI _____

ERGEINEN _____

SIGUEIDDTNHSI _____

ERINCDPOITS _____

Lesson 18: Spelling

Fill in the blanks with the correct spelling word. Be sure to spell it correctly!

The art _____ at the museum was a great field trip.

The incoming snow led to the meeting's _____.

Our _____ guest was the mayor.

Not to _____ you, but there's lettuce in your teeth.

The item's _____ said it was brand new.

The project _____ said the build was on schedule.

The firemen worked hard to _____ the flame.

The _____ of the hoop was smaller than the ball.

The species was nearly _____, but made a comeback.

I wasn't trying to _____, it was just a surprise.

The ants began to _____ the crumbs.

The race is _____ due to rain.

Is _____ a good system of government?

It is _____ to me that God exists.

You don't need to yell to _____ your point.

The firework display was _____!

This _____ has way too strong of a scent for me.

She is _____ tired after her long weekend.

Play hangman! See if you can figure out your spelling words in ten guesses or less. Cross out letters you've guessed to help yourself keep track. The words are in the Lesson Guide.

A B C D E F G H I J K L M N O P Q R S T U V W X Y Z

— — — — — — — — — — — —

A B C D E F G H I J K L M N O P Q R S T U V W X Y Z

— — — — — — — — — — — —

A B C D E F G H I J K L M N O P Q R S T U V W X Y Z

— — — — — — — — — — — —

A B C D E F G H I J K L M N O P Q R S T U V W X Y Z

— — — — — — — — — —

A B C D E F G H I J K L M N O P Q R S T U V W X Y Z

— — — — — — — — —

A B C D E F G H I J K L M N O P Q R S T U V W X Y Z

— — — — — — — —

Lesson 20: Spelling

See how many words you can spell correctly now as they are read to you. Learn from any mistakes you make.

_____   _____

_____   _____

_____   _____

_____   _____

_____   _____

_____   _____

_____   _____

_____   _____

Lesson 21: Spelling

Fill in this crossword using the spelling words listed at the bottom. These are words from the spelling lists from lessons 6, 11, and 16.

absorb	bacteria	deceive
advice	biscuit	diameter
advise	bureau	encircle
analyze	commotion	evident
artificial	confetti	exhibit
authority	congratulations	

Fix the errors you find in the following paragraphs. There are ten mistakes.

Marie Curie or Madame Curie as she is known to many was a scientist in the late 19th and early 20th centurys. Born in Poland, she moved to France to continue her scientific studies and ended up marrying a physics professor. The pear worked together for the advancement of science particularly physics.

Marie Curie shattered glass ceilings all over the place. She co-earned a Nobel Prize in 1903, making her the first woman ever to earn won. She went on to earn another one as well. After her husbands death, she took his place as professor of physics. She was the first women to hold the position.

Madame Curie is most known for her work with radium. Although exposure to the element eventually killed her her research leads to advancements in x-ray machines, which improve lives daily, almost a century after her death.

Fix the errors you find in the following paragraphs. There are ten mistakes.

At the end of World War II, Germany, as well as its former capital of berlin, was divided between the Allies and Russia. In the post-war period many people emigrated from the Russian side of East Germany too help rebuild the Allie's West Germany. The economy of East Germany suffered greatly from the lack of labor. In order to keep people from emigrating, as well as to protect their communist society from Western influence East Germany built a guarded brick wall in 1961 and topped it with barbed wire.

The wall was an immediate publicity catastrophe for East Germany and communism as a hole. The wall itself along with the very public punishments of those who tried to cross it showcased the tyranny of communism. Under U.S. pressure, the wall came down on November 9 1989 and within three years, all but three communist nations had collapsed.

Fix the errors you find in the following paragraphs. There are ten mistakes.

Jesse Owens was the grandson of a slave. Born in September of 1913 in Alabama Jesse was the youngest of ten children. Along with 1.5 million other african american's who were part of the "Great Migration," his family left the segregated south when he was nine years old and moved to Ohio in search of better opportunities. It was in Ohio that Jesse became a track and field star.

He was only in high school when he gained national attention for tying the world record in the 100 yard dash. At a college track meat, it took him less than an hours' time to break three world records and tie a forth. Then at the 1936 Olympics Jesse Owens achieved a feat no Olympian had ever achieved up to that point when he earned four gold medals. Jesses' performance undermined Adolf Hitler's ridiculous claims about racial superiority.

If you could choose someone you know to be president, who would you pick and why?

_____

_____

_____

_____

_____

_____

_____

_____

_____

Writing Tip: Your writing will be more exciting to your readers if you vary your sentences in type (remember simple, compound, and complex?) and length.

Write a dialogue between the main character in a book you're reading and another person like a friend, mother, or teacher. Punctuate it properly.

_____

_____

_____

_____

_____

_____

_____

_____

Fix the errors you find in the following paragraphs. There are ten mistakes.

Philip Sousa was born in Washington D.C. the third of ten children. When he was thirteen his father enlisted him in the Marine Corps too keep him from joining a circus band. He started as an apprentice with the Marine Band, and then he moved on two a theatrical orchestra where he learned to conduct. He then returned to the Marine Band as a conductor, going on to lead "The President's Band" under five presidents.

Sousa went on to be a composer of marches, earning him the nickname "the American March King". His most famous marches include the following the U.S. National March called "The Stars and Stripes Forever" and "Semper Fidelis" the afficial march of the U.S. Marine Corps. He eventually conducted his own band, named the Sousa Band, which featured a new instrument that most every marching band today uses — the aptly named sousaphone.

Write an advertisement for the paper using the prompts from the Lesson Guide.

_____

_____

_____

_____

_____

_____

_____

_____

Fix the errors you find in the following paragraph. There are five mistakes.

Clive Staples Lewis is a well-known British author, most famous four his *Chronicles of Narnia* series of books. Through his Christian faith is evident throughout many of his writings C.S. Lewis actually left Christianity for atheism during his university years. However after years of intellectual wrestling Lewis returned to Christianity and became a great defender of the faith.

Identify the part of speech of the underlined word by writing it on the line.

That <u>jump</u> was the highest of the meet. _____

I'll let <u>myself</u> out. _____

I'd love to fly <u>among</u> the stars. _____

The <u>shining</u> sun blinded the driver. _____

That fruit salad <u>looks</u> delicious! _____

We're <u>very</u> late for the meeting! _____

Fix the errors you find in the following paragraphs. There are ten mistakes.

Leonardo da Vinci mite be one of the most underrated people in history. You probably know he was an artist particularly a painter and sculpter. But he excelled in many other areas as well. He was a scientist who specialized in anatomy geology and botany He was also a righter, a mathematician, a musician, an architect, an engineer, a cartographer, and an impressive inventor.

Da Vincis inventions were amazingly ahead of his thyme. He invented the predecessor to the modern-day tank centuries before cars were invented. He even invented a fully animated robot while living in the 1400s! But his most famous invention stemmed from his favorite area of study — aviation. His famous flying machine probably has his Renaissance neighbors thinking he was as batty as the winged night creatures he studied to design it!

You've just been elected president of the world. What will you do first? Why? How will you go about it?

_____

_____

_____

_____

_____

_____

_____

_____

_____

Writing Tip: If you're having trouble getting started with a writing assignment, use any number of brainstorming methods to jot down any ideas you have. Then the writing simply becomes stringing your ideas together and can flow much more quickly.

Fix the errors you find in the following paragraph. There are ten mistakes.

Mary Elizabeth Bowser was a slave during the 1800's. As a young woman, she was freed by her owner and sent to a Quaker school where she learned to read and right. Once the civil war began her kind, former owner asked if she would help the union by spying on the Confederacy.

To do this, Mary had to pretend to be dim-witted and uneducated. She also had to go back to being treated like a slave, a life she had largely gotten a way from. She was hired by Jefferson Davis, the president of the Confederacy. Using her position within his home, she would eavesdrop on conversations read private communication's and then relay the information to a fellow spy who posed as a baker making regular bread deliveries. More than 100 years later, Mary was inducted into the U.S. Army Military Intelligence Corps Hall of Fame for her efforts.

Fix the errors you find in the following paragraph. There are ten mistakes.

James Weldon Johnson was an african american born in the late 1800's to a society focused on segregating his people. However he knew very few boundaries in his life. He was able to get a college education, and he went on to be a grammar school principal. In 1897 he became the first African American to pass the bar exam in Florida.

A few years later James and his brother together rote the song "Lift Every Voice and Sing", which eventually became the official anthem of the National Association for the Advancement of Colored People (or the NAACP). President Roosevelt appointed Johnson to diplomatic positions in Nicaragua and Venezuela.

In a society that largely saw African Americans as subpar James Johnson defied the odds and lived an extrordinary life.

Lesson 34: Writing – Friendly Letter

Language Arts 7

Do you remember how to write a friendly letter? Be sure to include the heading, salutation, body, closing, and signature.

_____

_____

_____

_____

_____

_____

_____

_____

_____

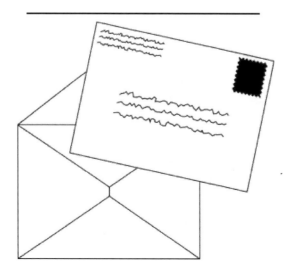

Fix the errors you find in the following paragraph. There are five mistakes.

The discovery of gold in California in 1848 changed the scope of many peoples lifes. Thousands migrated west, dreaming of the wealth that weighted beyond the horizon. Unfortunately, many dreamers lost everything. The cost of the supplies and the journey west squelched many dreams, before they really got started. Many even lost there lives chasing the riches.

Answer the following questions by selecting your choice from the answers given.

Which of the following sentences is an interrogative sentence?

a. I'm not sure what you're asking.   b. Please clarify your question.

c. Are you hungry?   d. I guess it's time for lunch.

What is the complete subject of this sentence? *Mary's teacher praised her efforts.*

a. Mary's teacher   b. Mary   c. praised   d. praised her efforts

What is the complete predicate of the same sentence?

a. Mary's teacher   b. Mary   c. praised   d. praised her efforts

Choose the simple subject and simple predicate of the same sentence.

a. Mary/efforts   b. teacher/praised   c. her/efforts

Lesson 36: Writing - Essay

Use this organizing chart to map out your five paragraph essay.

Topic:		
Introductory paragraph:		
Paragraph 2	Paragraph 3	Paragraph 4
Main idea:	Main idea:	Main idea:
Supporting Details	Supporting Details	Supporting Details
Concluding paragraph:		

Lesson 40: Editing Checklist

Read through your essay and fix any mistakes. Here is an editing checklist. Aim for a check mark in each box.

Introduction
- ☐ My introduction begins with an attention grabber.
- ☐ My introduction has at least three sentences.
- ☐ My introduction ends with the main idea of my essay.

Body
- ☐ The body of my essay has at least three paragraphs.
- ☐ Each paragraph of the body starts with a topic sentence.
- ☐ Each paragraph of the body has at least three supporting sentences.
- ☐ Each paragraph of the body has a conclusion sentence.

Conclusion
- ☐ My conclusion has at least three sentences.
- ☐ My conclusion restates my main idea.
- ☐ My conclusion answers the question, "So what?"

Unity
- ☐ My essay flows well and makes sense.
- ☐ My essay uses connecting words to transition between paragraphs.
- ☐ My essay is interesting.

Subject Matter
- ☐ My essay has different sentences – short, long, compound, complex.
- ☐ My essay uses descriptive words.
- ☐ All parts of my essay support my main idea.

Grammar/Mechanics
- ☐ All words are spelled correctly.
- ☐ There are no grammatical mistakes.
- ☐ There are no punctuation errors.
- ☐ There are no fragments.
- ☐ There are no run-on sentences.

Lesson 41: Writing - Design

Design a t-shirt for yourself that you would wear every day for a week so that everyone would see what it says and what's on it. Use the lines to brainstorm phrases and designs and the box to draw the actual t-shirt.

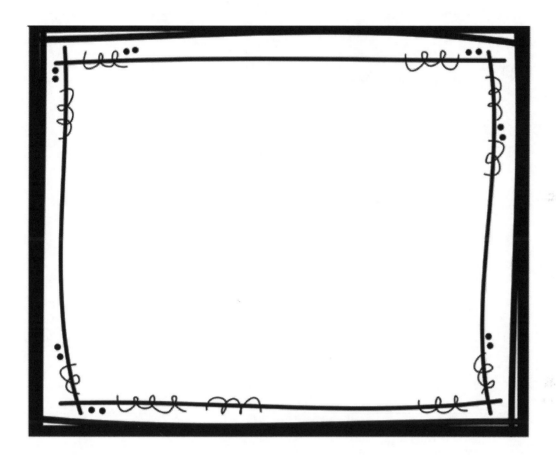

_____

_____

_____

_____

Lesson 43: Parts of Speech

Which part of speech is each of the listed words? Write your choice on the line beside each word.

quickly _____   curly _____

running _____   them _____

thick _____   very _____

horse _____   was _____

among _____   inch _____

us _____   long _____

basket _____   often _____

it _____   green _____

is _____   beside _____

myself _____   El Paso _____

tomorrow _____   lovely _____

under _____   prance _____

Lesson 44: Parts of Speech

Write the part of speech for the underlined word in each sentence.

The <u>hockey</u> puck flipped over the goal line. _____

Will you join me on a morning <u>run</u>? _____

That taco salad <u>looks</u> delicious. _____

Have you <u>ever</u> had raw sushi? _____

The cat is <u>beneath</u> the coffee table. _____

Why don't you grab a <u>quick</u> snack? _____

The dishes won't be washing <u>themselves</u>. _____

I can't <u>wait</u> for summer vacation. _____

Look <u>out</u> the window at that rainbow! _____

The big <u>drink</u> spilled all over the van. _____

This store is in such a <u>remote</u> place. _____

You need a <u>haircut</u>. _____

We should leave <u>soon</u> to get there on time. _____

Choose the correct form of the possessive for each sentence.

The _____ toys were scattered all over the house.

childrens'   children's   childrens's

_____ glasses fell. Louis couldn't find them.

Louis'   Louis's   Loui's

All of the _____ voices rose in harmony.

peoples'   peoples's   people's

The dog kept chasing _____ tail.

it's   its

The one _____ hair is longer than the hair of the other two ____.

girl's/girls'   girls'/girl's   girl's/girls

Fill in the plurals of the words below.

bus _____   mosquito _____

roof _____   deer _____

shelf_____   cheek_____

batch_____   mix _____

Fix the errors you find in the following paragraphs. There are ten mistakes.

Hedy Lamarr was an incredibly popular actress in the 1930's and 1940's. She had rolls opposite such popular stars as Clark Gable and Jimmy Stewart. Hedy was known as "The Most Beautiful Woman in Film" by her contemporaries.

However Hedy Lamarr was also incredibly intelligent. In 1942 along with her composer friend George Antheil Hedy patented what she called the "Secret Communication System". It was originally concocted to solve an issue in World War II where the Nazis were decoding messages and blocking signals from radio-controlled missiles. It involved changing radio frequencies so that enemies couldn't detect the messages in the first place. The later invention of the transistor catapulted Hedys' invention into practical space, and it is still used today in both military applications as well as sell phone technologys.

Write a summary of the story of Little Red Riding Hood.

_____

_____

_____

_____

_____

Fix the errors you find in the following paragraph. There are five mistakes.

Annie Oakley was forced to learn how to trap and shoot as early as age ate in order to support her family due to the death of her father. She became a fantastic shot while supporting her family and she went on to join Buffalo Bills Wild West show. Annie became a world-renowned rifle sharpshooter one of the best of all time. It is believed that she taught more than 15,000 woman to shoot a gun.

Fix the errors you find in the following paragraphs. There are ten mistakes.

In the 1950's, the space race was hot particularly between the united states and the Soviet Union. Each nation wanted to be the first one to do a certain thing in space. Some of the firsts were the first launch into space, first animal in space, first human in space, first human to orbit the earth, and others. When the Soviet Union started to get the lead in the race, the United States, in desperation, opened a project with one goal. They want to nuke the moon.

The precision was important. The whole point of nukeing the moon was making it visible to people. They planed to aim for the edge of the visible side of the moon. That way the cloud from the explosion would be illuminated by the sun and visible far and wide. Ultimately the project was abandoned do to concerns about contaminating space or the bomb detonating early and endangered the inhabitants of the earth.

Write what happens next in a favorite book of yours. Continue the story after the last chapter.

_____

_____

_____

_____

_____

_____

_____

_____

_____

_____

_____

Lesson 51: Crossword

Fill in the puzzle with the words below from *The Call of the Wild*.

courier   consternation   arduous

malinger   cadence   retrogression

indiscretion   fastidious   vicarious

belligerent

Lesson 52: Parts of Speech

Mark the part of speech for each word in the following sentence from *The Call of the Wild*: *He took Buck by the scruff of the neck, and though the dog growled threateningly, dragged him to one side and replaced Sol-leks.*

He	took	Buck	by

the	scruff	of	the

neck,	and	though	the

dog	growled	threateningly,	dragged

him	to	one	side

and	replaced	Sol-leks.

Use this sentence to answer the following questions: *The general tone of the team picked up immediately.*

What's the simple subject of the sentence? _____

What's the complete subject? _____

What's the predicate? _____

Lesson 53: Spelling

Find the words from *The Call of the Wild* in the word search below.

```
N W B Y P S N Z W D N T Y C T Y A C D E
J L U G U B R I O U S L Y D U I O D N P
Y O C R S M Q U H S C Y K X V V X C C Y
J K B A C C Z S E C C X S U Y N D Q N J
O N H G O D O T O N X C P G Y D D Y L X
H Y J A N E A M E L S S C O E M S O K E
O D A Z V M K I P G I X V R R E Y H A N
K O J B U C L G B E U D E K A W T I H E
M S I X L I O F P T L D A A S Y M E J R
S M K N S L K V B F N L V R R Q S Q O J
O I J E I I W T E U O F E B I O A O T G
N S R G V Q K S O T F R Q D R T V B P D
X O J F E C T L R G E J E O Z C Y D M D
U P U B Z D F V E I M D M V F Q A U B N
A X B Y T S Y I M N P E S Q A M Y R G U
R V E P S O M T N D H L L R D L Q A C J
W U F I Z H J D A E C Y I H E P U T V R
S D E L U G E D N P F B R E V S U E G A
P W B B R Q Q I T S F K O C L P U Z D F
F B C O D B L Q E M T S F L V B A W L D
```

morose   forevalued   deluged

remnant   solidarity   coveted

compelled   mates   floundered

convulsive   obdurate   lugubriously

                  resiliency

Answer the questions about the sentence from *The Call of the Wild* below.

Thirty days from the time it left Dawson, the Salt Water Mail, with Buck and his mates at the fore, arrived in Skaguay.

What is the subject of the sentence? _____

What is one prepositional phrase in the sentence? _____

_____

Remember that **gerunds** are *ing* words that function as nouns. Write three sentences using gerunds.

_____

_____

_____

_____

_____

Write for at least 15 minutes. Use a separate sheet of paper if you need more space.

_____

_____

_____

_____

_____

_____

_____

_____

_____

_____

_____

_____

_____

Lesson 56: Idiom Hangman

Play idiom hangman with someone! See if you can figure out these idioms in ten guesses or less. You might start with vowels or letters that are more common. Play with a sibling, parent, or friend to let you know if you're guessing correctly.

A B C D E F G H I J K L M N O P Q R S T U V W X Y Z

_ _

A B C D E F G H I J K L M N O P Q R S T U V W X Y Z

_ _ _ _ _ _ _ __ _ _ _ _ _ _ _ _ _ _

A B C D E F G H I J K L M N O P Q R S T U V W X Y Z

_ _ _ _ _ _ _ _ _ _ _ _ _ _ _ _ _

A B C D E F G H I J K L M N O P Q R S T U V W X Y Z

_ _ _ _ _ _ _ _ _ _ _ _ _ _ _ _

A B C D E F G H I J K L M N O P Q R S T U V W X Y Z

'

_ _ _ _ _ _ _ _ _ _ _ _ _ _ _ _ _ _

A B C D E F G H I J K L M N O P Q R S T U V W X Y Z

_ _ _ _ _ _ _ _ _ _ _ _ _ _ _

Find the words from *The Call of the Wild* in the word search below.

```
A  J  V  H  X  R  C  J  C  V  K  A  Z  Y  B
H  L  N  W  T  I  L  C  H  S  B  O  C  X  O
G  A  E  A  M  P  W  Q  M  U  U  D  W  J  R
Q  M  U  S  Q  D  D  S  C  N  E  Y  K  L  A
W  D  O  N  D  D  Y  E  S  T  T  S  S  Z  M
R  E  Y  N  C  X  B  K  A  I  X  H  X  G  S
C  L  Z  H  O  H  N  R  C  V  A  R  Y  K  H
A  L  W  R  Z  A  E  A  R  P  L  O  D  U  A
M  C  A  U  L  T  N  S  E  B  X  U  C  T  C
D  P  M  F  I  I  X  I  V  B  O  D  A  U  K
J  H  L  L  T  S  E  B  E  T  T  E  U  J  L
A  Z  B  R  B  K  G  L  J  A  V  D  L  G  E
I  O  E  V  V  P  Z  M  W  O  E  B  D  H  L
T  P  G  R  I  O  T  O  U  S  L  Y  I  U  Q
O  O  U  O  G  E  P  F  H  A  N  N  P  A  P
```

haunches	shrouded
paroxysms	pertinacity
obliterated	riotously
flanks	ramshackle

In each group of three, fill in the circle beside the sentence that contains the gerund. Underline it.

○ The rising smoke clouded the horizon.
○ Much adventure can be found while reading books.
○ Smiling at them, she made her way into the room.

○ Blowing bubbles in the yard is Ella's favorite activity.
○ Clara soaked in the tub to sooth her writhing muscles.
○ The tinkling ice made music in the glass.

○ Garret was blinded by all of the flashing cameras.
○ The speeding racecars were a blur.
○ Raising children can be exhausting.

○ The twirling baton fell to the ground.
○ Killing the bug made Andrew feel powerful.
○ Her growling stomach told her it was lunch time.

○ Eating ice cream in the car can be messy.
○ Her hacking cough kept her up all night.
○ Natalie was enthralled by the flapping of the butterfly's wings.

○ Matthew was made dizzy by the spinning fan.
○ The leaping ballerinas were fun to watch.
○ Caleb was excited about baking the cookies.

○ Giggling babies are the cutest.
○ The bouncing ball rolled down the hill
○ Singing is Wyatt's favorite hobby.

Write five gerund sentences.

_____

_____

_____

_____

_____

_____

_____

_____

Did You Know?: Gerunds and participles are so closely related that the authors of the *Cambridge Grammar of the English Language* just call the –ing form the "gerund-participle." The two words carry over from the Latin where they had different forms, making two names necessary.

Lesson 60: Writing

Write for at least 15 minutes. Use a separate sheet of paper if you need more space.

_____

_____

_____

_____

_____

_____

_____

_____

_____

_____

_____

_____

_____

Rewrite the ending of a book you've recently read.

_____

_____

_____

_____

_____

_____

_____

_____

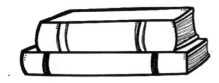 

Lesson 65: Editing Checklist

Read through your personal response and fix any mistakes. Here is a list of things to keep track of as you edit. Aim for a check mark in each box.

Introduction
☐ My introduction begins with an attention grabber.
☐ My introduction has at least three sentences.
☐ My introduction ends with the main idea of my paper.

Body
☐ The body of my paper has at least two key points.
☐ Each paragraph of the body starts with a topic sentence.
☐ Each paragraph of the body has at least three supporting sentences.
☐ Each paragraph of the body has a conclusion sentence.

Conclusion
☐ My conclusion has at least three sentences.
☐ My conclusion restates my main idea.
☐ My conclusion answers the question, "So what?"

Unity
☐ My paper flows well and makes sense.
☐ My paper uses transition words.
☐ My paper is interesting.

Subject Matter
☐ My paper has different sentences – short, long, compound, complex.
☐ My paper uses descriptive words.
☐ All parts of my paper support my main idea.

Grammar/Mechanics
☐ All words are spelled correctly.
☐ There are no grammatical mistakes.
☐ There are no punctuation errors.
☐ There are no fragments.
☐ There are no run-on sentences.

Lesson 66: Spelling - Crossword

Fill the words into the crossword puzzle using the letter clues and length of the words to help you.

calendar   mischievous
enthusiasm   mysterious
inconceivable   receive
inquiring   thief
interesting

Lesson 67: Punctuation and Capitalization

Answer the following grammar questions.

An interrogative sentence ends with a _____.

Is this sentence properly written? *"Kate" said Mom "please calm down."*
           a. yes   b. no

Apostrophes are used to show _____.

a. possession   b. missing letters   c. both

Circle the punctuation marks used incorrectly in this sentence. *A lot of families have more than four children; for example, the Smith's, Johnson's, and Chan's.*

An imperative sentence would never end in a _____.

Which of these sentences uses an apostrophe correctly?

    a.   The three girls' showed up late to class.
    b.   My dog's names are Dusty and Snickers.
    c.   Alabama's capital is Montgomery.
    d.   The church'es services let out early.

When you have a quotation inside of a quotation, you should use _____.

a.   double quotes around single quotes   b. italics   c. commas

When you have a list of three or more items, you should use _____.

a.   colons   b. conjunctions   c. commas

Which of these is *not* a proper use of a hyphen?

a.   great-grandfather   b. thir-teen   c. thirty-three

Lesson 68: Participle Phrases

In the following sentences, underline the participle phrases and circle what they are modifying.

Getting home on time, she raced inside.

Finishing the last lap, he raised his arms in victory.

Panting, the dog circled his bed and flopped down.

Glancing out the window, they noticed the rainbow.

Shooting the puck hard, Matthew scored a goal.

Saluting the flag, the choir sang the national anthem.

Gathering his things, Braden left for home.

Turning on his siren, the police officer chased the speeder.

In the following sentences, underline the gerund or the participle. On the line, write G if the underlined word is a gerund or P if it's a participle.

Arriving early is important to me. _____

Whistling while he worked, Daniel got the job done. _____

Showing his badge, the man was allowed to enter. _____

Singing is Sarah's favorite activity. _____

Eliana prefers dancing. _____

Noticing the deer in the road, Mom hit the brakes. _____

Tripping on his own two feet was Jake's specialty. _____

Standing tall, Jessica prepared to give her speech. _____

Write three sentences with participle phrases. Then rewrite them so that they contain gerunds instead.

1. _____

_____

2. _____

_____

3. _____

_____

1. _____

_____

2. _____

_____

3. _____

_____

Lesson 70: Writing

Write a short story with at least one gerund and one participle.

_____

_____

_____

_____

_____

_____

_____

_____

_____

_____

Lesson 71: Nouns

Answer the following grammar questions.

The subject is who or what the sentence is about.

        a. yes   b. no

Most nouns ending -y preceded by a vowel use -ies to make them plural.

        a. yes   b. no

The preposition of a sentence tells what happens in the sentence.

        a. yes   b. no

Which noun is the subject of this sentence? *Most children from Toronto love playing hockey.*

a. children   b. Toronto   c. love   d. hockey

What is the predicate of this sentence? *Most children from Toronto love playing hockey.*

a. children   b. Toronto   c. love   d. hockey

Find the nouns in this sentence and tell whether they are singular or plural: *The girl's dresses were hanging in a row.*

a. singular, plural, singular   b. plural, plural, singular

Find the nouns in this sentence and tell whether they are singular or plural: *The men's beards were groomed with clippers.*

a. singular, plural, plural   b. plural, plural, plural

Which of these is punctuated correctly?

a. The childrens' game took all afternoon, amusing them thoroughly.
b. The crowd's cheers erupted at the quick, powerful pitch.

Write two similes and two metaphors that describe aspects of your topic.

_____

_____

_____

_____

_____

_____

_____

_____

Writing Tip: Remember that similes and metaphors compare two unlike things. Metaphors call one thing the other. Similes use _like_ or _as_ to compare.

Write a paragraph of VIVID description.

_____

_____

_____

_____

_____

Write a list of specific verbs and great adjectives that can be used to describe your topic. Then list words that describe the smell, taste, sound, and feel of your topic.

Verbs

_____

_____

_____

Adjectives

_____

_____

_____

Smell

_____

_____

Taste

_____

_____

Sound

_____

Feel

_____

Lesson 76: Spelling

Find the words from *The Spy* in the word search below.

```
K J V H G P Q C P I C X B D D G E L
O O D L J S G E A E N A Q O N O L Z
W H W G R J M W H P T N F I O I O Q
Y I S V H I U O X M R U Z K S R Q J
O I R M L D D A X C T I L E X K U F
A O E B L G Q U G F U D C A F R E M
N I U B H L X N Q Q X C A I N K N U
N S O F T N I O O B O B Q Z O C C C
W Z F E N R U L A A H G G Q N U E L
L E L Z R N I E N S R V U S H M S F
D X Y E F L K Q F X N D Y T V I I X
X D N A O A I V Q P A P E U G R C N
W U O S X H C S K L N F U N I H F X
K N U L B R N Z C Y C G I H T S N F
P Q W T F G L G D Q K X I B F L N H
C Y N P I D I N P W E S X D W W Y F
Z W U N D P O R T E N T O U S Q Z M
K G L T W C O N T E M P T U O U S M
```

sublime   eloquence   portentous

ardently   petulance   contemptuous

unerring   capricious   soliloquizing

Fix the errors you find in the following paragraphs. There are ten mistakes.

Famines can be caused by a lack of food or by a lack of access to food. There are many different causes of famines. Extreme whether plant diseases and animals can all cause a lack of food. Even goverments can cut off access to food, resulting in famine.

Throughout history, weather has impacted our food supply. During horrible freezes or severe droughts food prices in the United states and other civilized nations can skyrocket to compensate for the lack of crops. But in other areas of the world weather causes true famine. Sometimes plants get diseases that cause them to die, creating the same lack of crops that weather can create. Animals and bugs can eat and destroy crops as well.

The most surprising cause of famine is tyrannical leaders who keep food from there own people. Today many systems are in place to prevent governments from harming there own people in this way.

Fix the errors you find in the following paragraphs. There are ten mistakes.

Manfred Albrecht Freiherr von Richthofen was a fighter pilot for germany during World War 1. He became one of the most famous fighter pilots of awl time throughout the course of the war. Painting his aircraft red lead him to be called by the nicknames "Red Fighter Pilot", "Red Battle Flyer", and, most famously, "Red Baron".

The Red Baron was likely the deadliest fighter pilot in the entire war. He was officially credited with eighty air combat victories before his death. At one point during combat, a hit to the head caused him temporary blindness. He recovered well enough to successfully make a rough landing of his plane. Eventually however his reputation made him a very sought-after target. Everyone wanted credit for bringing down the Red Baron and its still unclear who ultimately put the permanent end to his combat career.

Fix the errors you find in the following paragraphs. There are ten mistakes.

The city of Jerusalem is a fascinating place. It's historical background makes it a huge tourist location, drawing people from all parts of the world. But its biggest lure comes from its religious roots. In Hebrew, Yerushalayim means "foundation of peace". This name might be considered ironic. Since the city of Jerusalem is considered by three of the worlds' largest religions to be there religious center, it has been the reason for many wars over the centuries.

Christianity Judaism and Islam all consider Jerusalem to be important to they're religion. Over the years, Jerusalem has seen the rise and fall of the kingdom of Israel, the death and resurrection of Jesus Christ, the Crusades, and many other so-called "holy wars." In fact Israelis and Palestinians continue to fight over the writes to occupy Jerusalem too this day.

Lesson 85: Rubric

Use this writing rubric to assess your essay.

	Advanced	Proficient	Basic	Below Basic
Ideas/ Content	☐ Literary elements such as character, plot, setting, conflict, etc. are well-developed around a central idea	☐ Literary elements such as character, plot, setting, conflict, etc. are somewhat developed around a central idea	☐ Literary elements such as character, plot, setting, conflict, etc. are unclear or leave too many questions	☐ Literary elements such as character, plot, setting, conflict, etc. are confusing or missing
Organi- zation	☐ Paper has an effective, great introduction ☐ Conclusion provides resolution ☐ Structure is creative and clear	☐ Paper has a good introduction ☐ Conclusion mostly provides resolution ☐ Structure is mostly creative and clear	☐ Introduction is present but unclear ☐ Conclusion doesn't resolve the problem or tell us what happens next ☐ Structure is loose	☐ Introduction is confusing or non-existent ☐ Conclusion is hasty or non-existent ☐ No obvious structure
Voice	☐ Writer's voice adds interest ☐ Point of view is skillfully expressed	☐ Writer's voice is fitting ☐ Point of view is evident	☐ Writer's voice is repetitive ☐ Point of view is confusing	☐ No sense of voice ☐ Point of view is missing
Word/ Language Choice	☐ Words are used appropriately ☐ Figurative language included	☐ Words are used well ☐ Descriptions are satisfactory	☐ Words and meanings are vague ☐ Descriptions lacking	☐ Limited vocabulary utilized ☐ Descriptive language absent
Sentence Fluency	☐ Sentence structure enhances story ☐ Transitions used between sentences and paragraphs	☐ Varied sentence structure evident ☐ Transitions present	☐ Sentence structure repetitive ☐ Limited transitional phrases	☐ Rambling or awkward sentences ☐ Transitions missing

Fill in the blanks with your spelling words. You can have someone read them to you from the answer key.

I would _____ against speaking disrespectfully.

What has been your greatest _____ this year?

The sign said, "No _____."

Can you offer your _____ to that lady?

What's the postal _____ for Massachusetts?

Do you submit to those in _____?

The sponge will _____ the entire spill.

What's your _____ on this topic?

When I _____ the budget, I see a deficit.

I have a close _____ with my co-worker.

The state _____ building is located downtown.

The infection in my throat was caused by _____.

Do you put _____ on your applesauce?

The presidential _____ was successful.

I rode my _____ to work yesterday.

What's all the _____ outside?

The _____ winds its way by the beautiful park.

Of the bolded words, circle the one that matches the part of speech to the side of the sentence.

The **swarming gnats bothered** my **eyes**.   Adjective

I **guess** I'll **wash the** dishes **myself**.   Pronoun

Let's **go to** the **library tomorrow**.   Adverb

The frog **went** for a **swim in** the pond.   Noun

That dog looks hungry.   Verb

My **stomach** growled **loudly during** the **meeting**.   Preposition

The **sweetly** scented **lotion smelled** like **candy**.   Adverb

Today was a **very long** day.   Verb

The **top of** the window **was covered** in dust.   Preposition

The **giggly** girls **stayed up way** too late.   Adjective

His **love** was **boundless**.   Noun

Is that your **lost book**?   Pronoun

(continued on next page)

Use this page to brainstorm for your essay. Jot down as many things as you can think of.

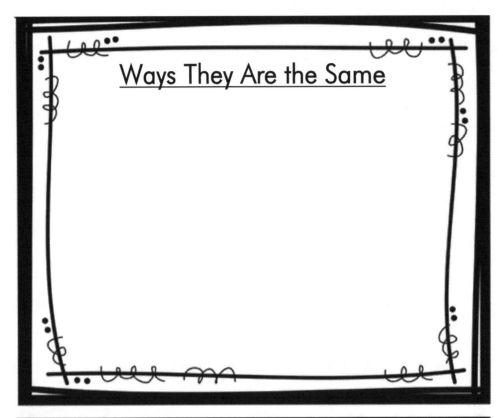

Ways They Are the Same

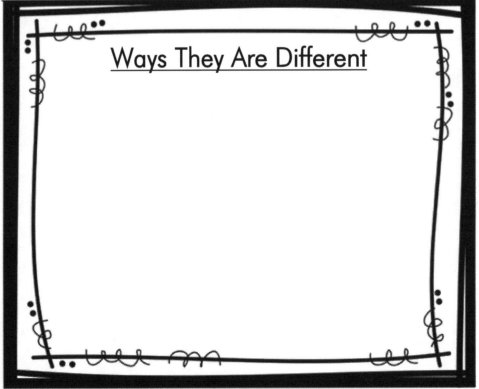

Ways They Are Different

Lesson 88: Compare and Contrast

Use this page along with your page from lesson 87 to figure out the three main points you are going to make. Show how they are the same and where they differ. Pair up three similarities and differences and write out three sentences.

_____

_____

_____

_____

_____

_____

_____

_____

_____

_____

Lesson 89: Concrete and Abstract Nouns

For each noun, circle whether it is concrete or abstract.

jewelry box

concrete   abstract

soccer ball

concrete   abstract

book

concrete   abstract

memory

concrete   abstract

America

concrete   abstract

magazine

concrete   abstract

friendship

concrete   abstract

bravery

concrete   abstract

calendar

concrete   abstract

pajamas

concrete   abstract

championship

concrete   abstract

lampshade

concrete   abstract

talent

concrete   abstract

Rebecca

concrete   abstract

uniform

concrete   abstract

future

concrete   abstract

Lesson 90: Plurals

For each noun, write the correct plural on the line.

yourself	_____	cherry	_____
stimulus	_____	ellipsis	_____
deer	_____	mouse	_____
cactus	_____	man	_____
crutch	_____	toy	_____
box	_____	moose	_____
child	_____	shelf	_____
hero	_____	pencil	_____
tray	_____	potato	_____
latch	_____	baby	_____
sheep	_____	calf	_____
bluff	_____	index	_____

Fix the errors you find in the following paragraphs. There are ten mistakes.

Abigail Adams was the wife of the first Vice President and second President of the United States John Adams. Though societal constraints of the day didn't allow Abigail to have any formal education she was self-educated and incredibly intelligent.

Abigail was a close confidant and advisor for her husband John. Many consider her to be one of the founders of the country because of the level of influence she had in his affairs. Historical letters written between the husband and wife show many intellectual discussions and are evidence of just how much John trusted his wife.

Abigail Adams believed in the importance of education and she home educated her five children. Her oldest son John Quincy Adams also went on to become President.

Rewrite the following paragraphs correctly. Be sure to proofread for errors in spelling, grammar, punctuation, capitalization, and usage.

Benjamin Franklin was a scientist inventor and writer. His most famous experiments dealt with electricity and he discovered many of it's governing laws. His work with electricity lead him to invent the lightening rod.

_____

_____

_____

_____

Franklin is considered won of americas Founding Fathers. He lived in england for many years as a representative of the colonist's who had gone to america. Though he never saw miliarty action during the revolutionary war, he did sign both the declaration of independance and the united states constitution.

_____

_____

_____

_____

Choose the correct pronoun to fill in the blank. If you need help, try to determine if the needed pronoun should be a subject or an object pronoun.

It was _____ who folded all of that laundry.

me   myself   I

My dad asked my brother and _____ to do our chores.

me   myself   I

Meg and _____ spent the entire day playing cards.

me   myself   I

My mom was not happy with _____ inviting   several friends over without asking.

me   myself   my

Between you and _____, that dinner could have been a lot better.

me   myself   I

_____ spent all night on the phone together.

She and Melanie   Melanie and her

_____ friendship is important to me.

Jennifer's and my   Me and Jennifer's   Myself and Jennifer's

Are you upset with _____ choosing of the movie?

me   myself   my

When it comes to haircuts, I like yours better than _____.

mine   mines   mine's

Read through your essay and fix any mistakes. Here is your editing checklist again. Remember to aim for a check mark in each box.

Introduction
☐ My introduction begins with an attention grabber.
☐ My introduction has at least three sentences.
☐ My introduction ends with the main idea of my essay.

Body
☐ The body of my essay has at least three paragraphs.
☐ Each paragraph of the body starts with a topic sentence.
☐ Each paragraph of the body has at least three supporting sentences.
☐ Each paragraph of the body has a conclusion sentence.

Conclusion
☐ My conclusion has at least three sentences.
☐ My conclusion restates my main idea.
☐ My conclusion answers the question, "So what?"

Unity
☐ My essay flows well and makes sense.
☐ My essay uses transition words.
☐ My essay is interesting.

Subject Matter
☐ My essay has different sentences – short, long, compound, complex.
☐ My essay uses descriptive words.
☐ All parts of my essay support my main idea.

Grammar/Mechanics
☐ All words are spelled correctly.
☐ There are no grammatical mistakes.
☐ There are no punctuation errors.
☐ There are no fragments.
☐ There are no run-on sentences.

Lesson 95: Pronouns • Rubric

_____

Choose the correct pronoun to fill in the blank. If you need help, try to determine
if the needed pronoun should be a subject or an object pronoun.

Are those glasses on the table _____ or mine?

       yours   your's   yours'

Grandma requested that you call _____ and Aunt Carrie.

     she   her

It was _____, that boy with the striped shirt, who threw
the ball.

     he   him

_____ wore heavy jackets on the ski trip.

   Her and I   She and I   Her and me

It could have been _____ who left the flowers on the porch.

     he   him

_____ share a locker.

   She and Becky   Becky and her

Dad sat between _____ and Ashley so they wouldn't talk.

     she   her

Ben realized that neither _____ nor Peter was ready for the
exam.

     he   him

Be sure to return to Mrs. Lovejoy what is _____.

     hers   her's   hers'

Lesson 95: Pronouns • Rubric

Use this writing rubric to assess your essay.

	Advanced	Proficient	Basic	Below Basic
Ideas/ Content	☐ Literary elements such as character, plot, setting, conflict, etc. are well-developed around a central idea	☐ Literary elements such as character, plot, setting, conflict, etc. are somewhat developed around a central idea	☐ Literary elements such as character, plot, setting, conflict, etc. are unclear or leave too many questions	☐ Literary elements such as character, plot, setting, conflict, etc. are confusing or missing
Organi-zation	☐ Paper has an effective, great introduction ☐ Conclusion provides resolution ☐ Structure is creative and clear	☐ Paper has a good introduction ☐ Conclusion mostly provides resolution ☐ Structure is mostly creative and clear	☐ Introduction is present but unclear ☐ Conclusion doesn't resolve the problem or tell us what happens next ☐ Structure is loose	☐ Introduction is confusing or non-existent ☐ Conclusion is hasty or non-existent ☐ No obvious structure
Voice	☐ Writer's voice adds interest ☐ Point of view is skillfully expressed	☐ Writer's voice is fitting ☐ Point of view is evident	☐ Writer's voice is repetitive ☐ Point of view is confusing	☐ No sense of voice ☐ Point of view is missing
Word/ Language Choice	☐ Words are used appropriately ☐ Figurative language included	☐ Words are used well ☐ Descriptions are satisfactory	☐ Words and meanings are vague ☐ Descriptions lacking	☐ Limited vocabulary utilized ☐ Descriptive language absent
Sentence Fluency	☐ Sentence structure enhances story ☐ Transitions used between sentences and paragraphs	☐ Varied sentence structure evident ☐ Transitions present	☐ Sentence structure repetitive ☐ Limited transitional phrases	☐ Rambling or awkward sentences ☐ Transitions missing

Lesson 96: Grammar Review

Answer the following questions by filling in the bubble beside your choice.

Which of these is a compound sentence?
○ I'm really hungry, so I should stop for lunch.
○ I'm not sure where I left my shoes.
○ Do you know what Jessica's phone number is, or not?

Which of these is a complex sentence?
○ Mrs. Johnson took us to the library, and then she went to the store.
○ When I grow up, I'm going to be a computer programmer.
○ We saw players, coaches, staff, and fans at the game.

Which of these is an independent clause?
○ If you have enough time
○ When I read books
○ I don't want to get up

Which of these is correct?
○ "Come here," I said!
○ "Come here!" I said.
○ "Come here." I said.

Her hair cascaded over her shoulders like a waterfall is an example of...
○ alliteration   ○ simile   ○ metaphor

Weather and *whether* are...
○ synonyms   ○ antonyms   ○ homophones

Love is war is an example of
○ alliteration   ○ simile   ○ metaphor

Almost and *nearly* are...
○ synonyms   ○ antonyms   ○ homophones

Lesson 97: Pronouns • Writing Organization

Choose the correct pronoun to fill in the blank.

It was _____ who cleaned up the kitchen.

      we   us

_____ whispering drew angry glances during the show.

      Us   Our

That bag belongs to _____ two.

      we   us

The teacher told _____ kids that we were really smart.

      we   us

The car with the red flaking paint is _____.

      ours   ours'   our's

We got all of the groceries in _____.

      ourselves   ourself   ourself's

Match the topic with the best organization for it by writing the corresponding letter on the line.

    A.   research report   B.   description
    C.   persuasive argument   D.   instructions

How to make a peanut butter and jelly sandwich   _____

Word picture of a sunset at the lake   _____

Need for lower college tuition   _____

Facts about internal combustion engines   _____

Choose the correct pronoun to fill in the blank.

The girls' kindness and _____ constant smiling warmed the hearts of the group leader.

their   them   they

_____ will be going to the diner if you'd like to join us.

They and I   I and them

Your seat is between _____.

Sammy and they   they and Sammy   Sammy and them

_____ and the other boys all loved to play basketball.

Their   Them   They

It was _____ who shoveled the snow off the deck.

their   them   they

When your brothers taunt you it's best to ignore _____ and their teasing.

their   them   they

Match the sentence to the type of writing by filling in the corresponding letter on the line.

A.   business report   B.   compare and contrast
C.   book review   D.   personal narrative

Vegetables are better for your health than fruit.   _____

Charlotte's Web is a charming book about a spider.   _____

The flat tire was just the beginning of my crazy day.   _____

The Senate recently passed a controversial bill.   _____

Choose the correct pronoun to fill in the blank.

My friend is so calm; I wish I was as calm as _____.

> her   she   herself

Jacob is a happy baby, and _____ giggling   brightens   a room.

> him   his   himself

CJ is good at soccer, but I hope to be better than _____.

> he   him   himself

_____ enjoyed our time at the fair.

> Brandon and me   Brandon and I

The director commended _____ kids on our production.

> us   we

I saw Alicia with that book, so I think it's _____.

> her's   hers'   hers

They all saved up enough money _____.

> theirselves   themselves   themselfs

Choose the more vivid word to complete the sentence.

The (tasty/mouth-watering) meal left us satisfied.

The (exhausting/hard) exercises strengthened my muscles.

My (panting/hot) dog needed a drink of water.

James was (mad/indignant) at the referee's call.

Tell whether the following sentences have pronoun reference errors.

Sophia said Alaina raced her to the mailbox and she won.

      yes   no

It says in the newspaper that there is a big parade this weekend.

      yes   no

Christy said that she needed to take a nap.

      yes   no

The girls used their crayons to make a big picture.

      yes   no

Choose six sentences from a recent writing assignment. Number the sentences, and fill in each column for each sentence. If you don't see a lot of variation in your writing, make some changes to make your writing more interesting.

Sentence Number	Number of Words	Sentence Type	Beginning Word	Connecting Word

Lesson 103: Plurals

Answer the questions about plurals by filling in the circle beside your choice.

The plural of "scenario" is...

○ scenarii   ○ scenarios   ○ scenarioes

The plural of "theory" is...

○ theories   ○ theorys   ○ theory

The plural of "thief" is...

○ thiefs   ○ thief   ○ thieves

The plural of "child" is...

○ childs   ○ children   ○ childes

The plural of "root" is...

○ root   ○ rootes   ○ roots

The plural of "curriculum" is...

○ curricula   ○ curriculums   ○ curriculi

Spell the plural form of the word on the line beside it.

parenthesis_____   berry   _____

mosquito_____   fox   _____

zero   _____   ox   _____

stimulus   _____   goose   _____

Fill in the circle beside the answer that best fits the blank.

This _____ meeting was a long one.

○ mornings   ○ morning's   ○ mornings'

The top _____ brackets were failing.

○ shelf's   ○ shelves   ○ shelfs'

The large assortment of _____ made my mouth water.

○ donut's   ○ donuts'   ○ donuts

Our _____ belt was squeaking loudly.

○ vans   ○ van's   ○ vans'

The three _____ lockers were all in a row.

○ boys   ○ boy's   ○ boys'

I can hear that _____ cries from here!

○ baby's   ○ babys'   ○ babies

The _____ purse was hanging off her shoulder.

○ women's   ○ woman's   ○ womens'

I don't have all of my _____ in a row.

○ ducks   ○ duck's   ○ ducks'

The _____ lids were bulging.

○ box's   ○ box'es   ○ boxes'

We rode our _____ to the mall.

○ bikes'   ○ bikes   ○ bike's

Lesson 105: Possessives

Fill in the circle beside the answer that best fits the blank.

This _____ keyboard has sticky keys.

  ○ computer's   ○ computers'

The _____ restroom had a long line.

  ○ women's   ○ womens'

Those _____ reports took the entire day.

  ○ student's   ○ students'

The _____ message was deceiving.

  ○ commercial's   ○ commercials'

The three _____ ringers all went off at once.

  ○ phone's   ○ phones'

Those _____ stems are all missing.

  ○ cherry's   ○ cherries'

Are you wearing _____ jeans?

  ○ men's   ○ mens'

The _____ tails were all bushy.

  ○ fox's   ○ foxes'

That _____ cheese is oozing.

  ○ sandwich's   ○ sandwiches'

The _____ engine startled the entire neighborhood.

  ○ motorcycle's   ○ motorcycles'

See if you can remember how to spell these previous spelling words as they are read to you from the Lesson Guide. Learn from any mistakes you make.

_____   _____

_____   _____

_____   _____

_____   _____

_____   _____

_____   _____

_____   _____

_____   _____

Lesson 107: Apostrophes

Fill in the circle beside the statement that applies to the underlined word.

The <u>Smith's</u> invited the entire neighborhood to their pool party.

⚪ The word is correct.　　　　⚪ No apostrophe is necessary.

I wish you <u>wouldn't</u> eat your cookies on the couch.

⚪ The word is correct.　　　　⚪ No apostrophe is necessary.

The <u>childrens'</u> game was noisy.

⚪ The word is correct.　　　　⚪ The word should be *children's*.

Our two <u>cities</u> are meeting for the championship.

⚪ The word is correct.　　　　⚪ The word should be *city's*.

That blue house on the corner is <u>our's</u>.

⚪ The word is correct.　　　　⚪ No apostrophe is necessary.

That red house next to it is <u>theirs'</u>.

⚪ The word is correct.　　　　⚪ No apostrophe is necessary.

<u>Jesse's</u> notebook was left in our van.

⚪ The word is correct.　　　　⚪ No apostrophe is necessary.

The <u>player's</u> jerseys had a patch in support of cancer research.

⚪ The word is correct.　　　　⚪ The word should be *players'*.

Our <u>friends'</u> leg is in a cast.

⚪ The word is correct.　　　　⚪ The word should be *friend's*.

The <u>tablet's</u> screen has a crack in it.

⚪ The word is correct.　　　　⚪ No apostrophe is necessary.

Lesson 108: Lose vs. Loose

Choose which word best fits the blank. Learn from any mistakes.

I don't want to _____ my glasses, but I need to take them off.
　○ lose　　　　　　　　　　○ loose

Gather up your _____ change, and see if it's enough for a treat.
　○ lose　　　　　　　　　　○ loose

The chain on my bike is _____.
　○ lose　　　　　　　　　　○ loose

Even if we _____ the game, we still get a second place trophy.
　○ lose　　　　　　　　　　○ loose

If we leave now, we'll _____ our place in line.
　○ lose　　　　　　　　　　○ loose

My little brother has his first _____ tooth.
　○ lose　　　　　　　　　　○ loose

I don't have any more baby teeth to _____.
　○ lose　　　　　　　　　　○ loose

Don't win the battle, only to _____ the war.
　○ lose　　　　　　　　　　○ loose

I always stretch to get _____ before a run.
　○ lose　　　　　　　　　　○ loose

That _____ lug nut needs to be tightened on the hubcap.
　○ lose　　　　　　　　　　○ loose

Lesson 109: Who vs. Whom

Choose which word best fits the blank. Learn from any mistakes.

The waitress _____ you requested is off tonight.

　　○ who　　　　　　　　　　○ whom

He is the man _____ we met last week.

　　○ who　　　　　　　　　　○ whom

_____ brought me this beautiful bouquet?

　　○ Who　　　　　　　　　　○ Whom

_____ are you taking to the park with you?

　　○ Who　　　　　　　　　　○ Whom

I haven't yet decided _____ should get the main part.

　　○ who　　　　　　　　　　○ whom

She is the lady _____ we were looking for.

　　○ who　　　　　　　　　　○ whom

Wait until I tell you _____ I saw at the grocery store!

　　○ who　　　　　　　　　　○ whom

_____ should I say is asking?

　　○ Who　　　　　　　　　　○ Whom

_____ should we ask to dinner?

　　○ Who　　　　　　　　　　○ Whom

I need a helper on _____ I can depend.

　　○ who　　　　　　　　　　○ whom

Lesson 111: Spellcheck

This paragraph contains five misspelled words. Can you figure out what they are and spell them correctly on the lines?

The United States House of Representatives is the lower chamber of the U.S. Congress. The Senate is the upper chamber. Together they make up the legislachur of the United States. The House of Representatives has a fixed number of 435 members, voted into office every to years. Each state gets a number of representatives in proportion to its population. The least populated states get only one representative, while the more populus states currently have over fifty. Representatives are spread around the state, speeking for different congressional districts that might have different needs or desires. The House votes on bills that have the potenchul to eventually become laws. The House of Representatives plays an important role in the checks and balances of the United States government.

_____   _____

_____   _____

_____

Lesson 112: Plurals and Possessives

Fill in the circle beside the answer that best fits the blank.

The _____ were intense.

   ○ exercises   ○ exercise's   ○ exercises'

The _____ smile was a bit creepy.

   ○ skeletons   ○ skeleton's   ○ skeletons'

Both of my _____ have flat tires.

   ○ bikes   ○ bike's   ○ bikes'

The two _____ pictures complemented each other.

   ○ posters   ○ poster's   ○ posters'

The _____ rungs were spaced twelve inches apart.

   ○ ladders   ○ ladder's   ○ ladders'

That _____ incline was difficult to climb.

   ○ hills   ○ hill's   ○ hills'

The three _____ heads popped up in unison.

   ○ squirrels   ○ squirrel's   ○ squirrels'

Neither of the two _____ were working.

   ○ microwaves   ○ microwave's   ○ microwaves'

That _____ numbers were faded.

   ○ keypads   ○ keypad's   ○ keypads'

Those _____ roofs make an interesting skyline.

   ○ buildings   ○ building's   ○ buildings'

Write for at least 10 minutes. Use a separate sheet of paper if you need more space.

_____

_____

_____

_____

_____

_____

_____

_____

_____

_____

_____

_____

Lesson 114: Plurals and Possessives

Fill in the circle beside the answer that best fits the blank.

The _____ weave hurt my eyes.

  ◯ carpets   ◯ carpet's   ◯ carpets'

The two _____ antlers were locked together.

  ◯ deers   ◯ deer's   ◯ deers'

The _____ decision was to build the park.

  ◯ peoples   ◯ people's   ◯ peoples'

The area _____ are closed.

  ◯ schools   ◯ school's   ◯ schools'

The four _____ hands all showed different times.

  ◯ clocks   ◯ clock's   ◯ clocks'

The _____ angles made it difficult to paint.

  ◯ ceilings   ◯ ceiling's   ◯ ceilings'

All four _____ rolled down the hill faster than we could run.

  ◯ balls   ◯ ball's   ◯ balls'

The _____ drawings showcased her talent.

  ◯ girls   ◯ girl's   ◯ girls'

The two _____ laces didn't match.

  ◯ shoes   ◯ shoe's   ◯ shoes'

The _____ wouldn't work because the _____ were dead.

◯ flashlights/batteries ◯ flashlight's/batteries ◯ flashlights'/batteries'

Write for at least 10 minutes. Use a separate sheet of paper if you need more space.

_____

_____

_____

_____

_____

_____

_____

_____

_____

_____

_____

_____

_____

Lesson 116: Possessives

Choose the correct form of the possessive for each sentence.

_____ car was a bright shade of red.

Cindy's   Cindys'   Cindies'

_____ car was a darker shade.

Chris'   Chris's   Chri's

The _____ department is downstairs.

mens   mens'   men's

The two _____ fins cut through the water towards us.

shark's   sharks'   sharks

The book landed on _____ spine.

its'   it's   its

The seven _____ windows were left open in the rain.

bus's   buses'   buses's

Your shearers shaved a lot of _____ wool.

sheep's   sheeps'   sheeps

My _____ names are Whisper and Mittens.

cats   cats'   cat's

The _____ feathers ruffled as it landed.

goose's   geeses'   geese's

That _____ antenae is broken.

radioes   radios'   radio's

Use this page to come up with the plan for your point of view story. Know what your story is going to be. Describe your two characters and how the story will differ.

_____

_____

_____

_____

_____

_____

_____

_____

_____

_____

Lesson 121: Spelling

See how many words you can spell correctly the first time as they are read to you from the Lesson Guide. Learn from any mistakes you make.

_____   _____

_____   _____

_____   _____

_____   _____

_____   _____

_____   _____

_____   _____

Lesson 122: Spelling - Unscramble

Language Arts 7

Unscramble your spelling words.

AABTFEICR   _____

THPILOSA   _____

CVNEGERIA   _____

NRIGEOF   _____

OIRYHFR   _____

UIMDH   _____

RNUGETAAE   _____

RFNALATG   _____

CHVAO   _____

INATINFGCSA   _____

SOPGNSGII   _____

NEYHEGI   _____

IOCREH   _____

IFEORTF   _____

INEUGNE   _____

SSAAHR   _____

AMGARRM   _____

FULYEQNTRE   _____

Fill in the blanks with the correct spelling word. Be sure to spell it correctly!

There is no _____ that you will win.

Did you just _____ that officer?

It would _____ Mother to know what you said.

Don't _____ a story to stay out of trouble.

The history museum is _____ to me.

Are we going to finish our game or do you _____?

It is so _____ outside this summer.

The rain is wreaking _____ on my hair.

Grandpa is being released from the _____ today.

Snow is a _____ concept to warmer climates.

The _____ foul cost the team the game.

It snows _____ in many northern states.

Her _____ act saved the puppy from being trapped.

The neighbor filed a _____ about the loud party.

The girls were caught _____ about their teacher.

The boy's kindness was _____.

Always check spelling and _____ in your papers.

Her _____ habits were pristine.

Lesson 124: Spelling - Hangman

Play hangman! See if you can figure out your spelling words in ten guesses or less. Cross out letters you've guessed to help yourself keep track. The words are in the Lesson Guide.

A B C D E F G H I J K L M N O P Q R S T U V W X Y Z

__ __ __ __ __ __ __ __ __

A B C D E F G H I J K L M N O P Q R S T U V W X Y Z

__ __ __ __ __ __ __

A B C D E F G H I J K L M N O P Q R S T U V W X Y Z

__ __ __ __ __ __ __

A B C D E F G H I J K L M N O P Q R S T U V W X Y Z

__ __ __ __ __ __ __ __

A B C D E F G H I J K L M N O P Q R S T U V W X Y Z

__ __ __ __ __ __

A B C D E F G H I J K L M N O P Q R S T U V W X Y Z

__ __ __ __ __ __ __ __

See how many words you can spell correctly now as they are read to you. Learn from any mistakes you make.

_____   _____

_____   _____

_____   _____

_____   _____

_____   _____

_____   _____

_____   _____

_____   _____

See how many words you can spell correctly the first time as they are read to you from the Lesson Guide. Learn from any mistakes you make.

_____   _____

_____   _____

_____   _____

_____   _____

_____   _____

_____   _____

_____   _____

Unscramble your spelling words.

ITNTIKGN   _____

LIACNDETI   _____

NSIFMUOA   _____

EYTALIIMMDE   _____

NTLELIETNGI   _____

NBRLEDCEII   _____

ELETTK   _____

DOLI   _____

CIONENNCE   _____

NELIVEJU   _____

ILOMIEZMBI   _____

TSIIRERBESLI   _____

DNGTJUEM   _____

TPLIYSOMSIBII   _____

CTNUSRORTI   _____

NNCNEOVTIEIN   _____

IEART   _____

LDIE   _____

Fill in the blanks with the correct spelling word. Be sure to spell it correctly!

My dance _____ taught us ballet.

Your mother is _____ a beautiful blanket.

The _____ robber was caught red-handed.

_____ hands lead to trouble.

My sister was _____ when I read her diary.

The tea _____ is whistling on the stove.

These cookies are absolutely _____.

Declaring his _____, the man walked away.

Stop blowing bubbles in your milk. It's so _____!

What an _____ sunset.

This detour is very _____.

Many people treat money as an _____.

We had to _____ his leg after he landed on it.

Do you know any _____ twins?

I need you to come here _____!

Use your best _____ when choosing.

The boy is so _____ he taught the teacher.

Finishing schoolwork can seem like an _____.

Play hangman! See if you can figure out your spelling words in ten guesses or less. Cross out letters you've guessed to help yourself keep track. The words are in the Lesson Guide.

A B C D E F G H I J K L M N O P Q R S T U V W X Y Z

___ ___ ___ ___ ___ ___ ___ ___ ___ ___ ___ ___

A B C D E F G H I J K L M N O P Q R S T U V W X Y Z

___ ___ ___ ___ ___ ___ ___

A B C D E F G H I J K L M N O P Q R S T U V W X Y Z

___ ___ ___ ___ ___

A B C D E F G H I J K L M N O P Q R S T U V W X Y Z

___ ___ ___ ___ ___ ___ ___ ___ ___ ___ ___

A B C D E F G H I J K L M N O P Q R S T U V W X Y Z

___ ___ ___ ___ ___ ___ ___

A B C D E F G H I J K L M N O P Q R S T U V W X Y Z

___ ___ ___ ___ ___ ___ ___ ___ ___ ___

Lesson 130: Spelling

Language Arts 7

See how many words you can spell correctly now as they are read to you. Learn from any mistakes you make.

Find and underline all of the infinitives in the following story.

We want to go to the park this afternoon. It's going to be a nice, sunny day. The temperature is hovering right around 70 degrees, a perfect day to swing in the breeze.

We're planning to take a picnic with us. My sister is going to eat a sandwich, but my brother prefers to have fruit salad. I think the fruit salad is just going to attract ants and bees, so I'll be sure to use bug spray before we head out to the park.

My favorite thing to do at the park is kick the ball around with my siblings. Hopefully this time my brother doesn't accidentally hit my sister in the face with the ball. No one needs to hear her shriek like that again! But I need to remind my brother to take some allergy medicine before we leave. Otherwise, he's going to sneeze for the rest of the day!

Lesson 132: Spelling

Find the words from *The Talisman* in the word search below.

```
K  L  D  I  Z  U  I  N  C  O  N  I  J  Y  T
O  A  A  Q  M  Z  A  T  J  R  O  L  W  N  V
I  U  H  X  U  I  E  V  U  K  S  Y  O  U  Q
L  R  P  Z  N  V  T  H  E  W  I  P  N  I
S  E  O  U  Y  Z  I  I  E  Z  T  W  Q  O  C
F  L  Y  H  C  C  W  G  G  A  R  Q  R  P  E
P  S  I  X  A  B  J  Y  C  A  D  L  L  L  U
J  Q  S  T  B  R  I  I  B  I  T  Y  C  Y  J
P  S  D  C  B  E  F  J  D  R  W  I  W  A  C
T  F  D  G  B  I  I  R  O  E  J  K  O  W  V
J  B  R  E  T  K  O  L  N  O  D  I  Z  N  R
L  Q  I  R  Q  S  K  I  M  Z  A  B  O  X  F
D  U  O  B  Y  Q  S  E  J  L  W  O  A  C  J
G  M  T  N  E  A  U  D  A  C  I  O  U  S  U
P  Y  L  S  M  F  S  U  J  B  Q  G  T  P  F
```

audacious   laurels   mitigation

mortification   sinewy   sordid

                  taciturn

Lesson 133: Spelling

Fill in the blanks with your spelling words. You can have someone read them to you from the answer key.

The park included three _____ of luscious grass.

The seatbelt was _____ to fit her small waist.

The _____ kept her warm when the heat went out.

What's your _____ of this situation?

This _____ sweetener has an aftertaste.

Are you _____ certain you turned off the stove?

What has been your greatest _____ this year?

Iris picked a lovely _____ of wildflowers.

_____ are in order for the winners.

The crowd threw _____ as the newlyweds ran past.

The _____ of California is Sacramento.

Chase likes to put honey on his morning _____.

Sara put her jewelry box on top of the _____.

It seems a mouse was the cookie thief _____.

The _____ was fierce at the spelling bee.

Not to _____ you, but there's lettuce in your teeth.

The item's _____ said it was brand new.

The project _____ said the build was on schedule.

Lesson 134: Gerunds and Infinitives

Does the sentence need a gerund or an infinitive? Write the proper form of the word in parentheses on the line in the sentence, and then tell whether it is a gerund (g) or infinitive (i) on the line at the end.

Are you free _____ this weekend?   _____
(work)

I expect you _____ up that spill.   _____
(clean)

I don't mind _____ to you while you clean.   _____
(read)

Can you tell me how _____ to the library?   _____
(get)

I can't picture Todd _____ to the music.   _____
(dance)

The girls are _____ on the trampoline.   _____
(jump)

Do you plan _____ to the park?   _____
(go)

Consider _____ Lincoln for your paper.   _____
(research)

Are you _____ the marathon this weekend?   _____
(run)

We chose _____ the 5K.   _____
(walk)

Write a song.

_____

_____

_____

_____

_____

_____

_____

_____

Write one of each of these types of sentences: declarative, interrogative, exclamatory, imperative, simple, compound, complex, sentence using *however*, sentence using a semicolon.

_____

_____

_____

_____

_____

_____

_____

_____

_____

_____

Each of the sentences below contains a dangling modifier. Rewrite each sentence so that the participle phrase modifies the noun it should.

Covered in delicious, sugary syrup, mother served the towering pile of pancakes.

_____

_____

_____

Soaked to the bone, everything Haylee touched became wet as well.

_____

_____

_____

Running all day and night, we called a handyman to fix the heater.

_____

_____

_____

Choose the sentence of each group that is formatted correctly by filling in the circle next to your choice.

○ Straining to see the stage, the seats were too far back for my nearsighted sister.

○ The seats were too far back for my nearsighted sister, who was straining to see the stage.

○ The seats, too far back for my nearsighted sister, were straining to see the stage.

○ Sweetly smiling, the bouquet was received by my mother.

○ The bouquet was received by my mother, sweetly smiling.

○ Sweetly smiling, my mother received the bouquet.

○ Kicking the ball, my brother broke the kitchen window.

○ Kicking the ball, the kitchen window was broken by my brother.

○ Breaking the kitchen window, the ball was kicked by my brother.

○ Sitting down to dinner, the wonderful aroma made us all drool.

○ The wonderful aroma, sitting down to dinner, made us all drool.

○ We all drooled at the wonderful aroma as we sat down to dinner.

Underline each sentence in the following story that has a dangling or misplaced modifier.

Last weekend, my family went on a camping trip. Arriving at our destination early, the campsite wasn't ready yet. Deciding to go for a walk, we hiked around the campground to get the lay of the land. We figured it'd be nice to know what to expect from our weekend. Spotting a creek, my camera wouldn't focus well enough to get a picture of the meandering water. Swallowing my disappointment, my dad called me over to check out the pool. Noticing the slide, I perked up a little. I love a good pool slide.

At long last, we got the text that our campsite was ready. Setting up our tent, the dog started barking. Following his gaze, the park ranger was seen coming up to our site. Informing us of an issue with the site we were on, the ranger offered a free upgrade to a fully loaded camper. Needless to say, we had a fabulous weekend roughing it in the woods!

If you could heal 12 people, and only 12, who would you heal and why?

_____

_____

_____

_____

_____

_____

_____

_____

_____

Writing Tip: Don't forget to vary your writing using transition words; complex, compound, and simple sentences; different beginnings; exciting words; etc. Think of your reader while you're writing and make it interesting!

Lesson 141: Spellcheck

This paragraph contains five misspelled words. Can you figure out what they are and spell them correctly on the lines?

When the original American colonists decided to revolt against British rule, there were many who were convinced the endeavor was destined for failure. Of course, without the benefit of hindsight, that feels like a fair assessment. After all, the colonists had an enormous undertaking to acomplish. They were attempting to addopt an entirely original form of government. They needed to addhere to a whole new adsortment of laws and legislations. While modern American leaders might agravate the world from time to time, the fledgling band of revolutionaries that started the United States achieved an incredible feat.

_____   _____

_____   _____

_____

Use this excerpt from Mark Twain's *The Prince and the Pauper* to answer the questions in lessons 142-144.

One January day, on his usual begging tour, he tramped despondently up and down the region round about Mincing Lane and Little East Cheap, hour after hour, bare-footed and cold, looking in at cook-shop windows and longing for the dreadful pork-pies and other deadly inventions displayed there—for to him these were dainties fit for the angels; that is, judging by the smell, they were—for it had never been his good luck to own and eat one. There was a cold drizzle of rain; the atmosphere was murky; it was a melancholy day. At night Tom reached home so wet and tired and hungry that it was not possible for his father and grandmother to observe his forlorn condition and not be moved—after their fashion; wherefore they gave him a brisk cuffing at once and sent him to bed. For a long time his pain and hunger, and the swearing and fighting going on in the building, kept him awake; but at last his thoughts drifted away to far, romantic lands, and he fell asleep in the company of jewelled and gilded princelings who live in vast palaces, and had servants salaaming before them or flying to execute their orders. And then, as usual, he dreamed that HE was a princeling himself.

All night long the glories of his royal estate shone upon him; he moved among great lords and ladies, in a blaze of light, breathing perfumes, drinking in delicious music, and answering the reverent obeisances of the glittering throng as it parted to make way for him, with here a smile, and there a nod of his princely head.

And when he awoke in the morning and looked upon the wretchedness about him, his dream had had its usual effect—it had intensified the sordidness of his surroundings a thousandfold. Then came bitterness, and heart-break, and tears.

(continued on next page)

Based on this excerpt, Tom must be...
- ○ The prince
- ○ The pauper
- ○ Neither

According to the third paragraph, Tom's dreams made his reality...
- ○ sweeter
- ○ like a dream
- ○ even more horrible
- ○ intense

We get the idea in this excerpt that Tom is...
- ○ a poor beggar child
- ○ happy with his childhood
- ○ lonely
- ○ a good student

Read this line from the first paragraph: *he tramped <u>despondently</u> up and down the region* – in which of these words does the suffix –ly mean the same as it does in the word *despondently*?
- ○ curly
- ○ melancholy
- ○ giggly
- ○ fly

Tom was kept awake by...
- ○ fighting
- ○ hunger
- ○ pain
- ○ all of these

Reread the excerpt from Mark Twain's *The Prince and the Pauper* in lesson 142 and then answer the questions.

Tom's father and grandmother were…
- ○ uncaring
- ○ happy that Tom was forlorn
- ○ beggars
- ○ moved by his tired, wet condition

Based on the context, "*dreadful pork-pies and other deadly inventions*" was describing food Tom believed to be…
- ○ poisoned
- ○ disgusting
- ○ delicious
- ○ too expensive

A good description of the weather in the excerpt would be…
- ○ cheerful
- ○ glum
- ○ nervous
- ○ indifferent

The word *execute* at the end of the first paragraph means…
- ○ kill
- ○ carry out
- ○ write down
- ○ hang

According to the third paragraph, a good synonym for Tom's surroundings would be…
- ○ disgusting
- ○ pleasant
- ○ congenial
- ○ boring

Lesson 144: Reading Comprehension

Reread the excerpt from Mark Twain's *The Prince and the Pauper* in lesson 142 and then answer the questions.

That Tom *"fell asleep in the company of jewelled and gilded princelings"* means that he...
- ○ really was rich and just pretended to be poor
- ○ was sleeping somewhere other than his home
- ○ was dreaming
- ○ was a prince

Which of these words from the story uses a suffix to change an adjective into a noun?
- ○ wretchedness
- ○ murky
- ○ delicious
- ○ princelings

According to the excerpt, Tom's dream of being a prince was...
- ○ the first one he'd had
- ○ unusual
- ○ a normal occurrence
- ○ we don't have information about it

Judging from the context, a good synonym for the word *"obeisance"* would be...
- ○ annoyance
- ○ ignorant
- ○ intelligence
- ○ respect

Why was Tom in tears at the end of the excerpt?
- ○ He was poor.
- ○ He wished to be a prince.
- ○ His dream had made his reality seem that much worse.
- ○ all of the above

Use this excerpt from Charles Dickens' *Great Expectations* to answer the questions in lessons 145-147.

This was very uncomfortable, and I was half afraid. However, the only thing to be done being to knock at the door, I knocked, and was told from within to enter. I entered, therefore, and found myself in a pretty large room, well lighted with wax candles. No glimpse of daylight was to be seen in it. It was a dressing-room, as I supposed from the furniture, though much of it was of forms and uses then quite unknown to me. But prominent in it was a draped table with a gilded looking-glass, and that I made out at first sight to be a fine lady's dressing-table.

Whether I should have made out this object so soon if there had been no fine lady sitting at it, I cannot say. In an arm-chair, with an elbow resting on the table and her head leaning on that hand, sat the strangest lady I have ever seen, or shall ever see.

She was dressed in rich materials,—satins, and lace, and silks,—all of white. Her shoes were white. And she had a long white veil dependent from her hair, and she had bridal flowers in her hair, but her hair was white. Some bright jewels sparkled on her neck and on her hands, and some other jewels lay sparkling on the table. Dresses, less splendid than the dress she wore, and half-packed trunks, were scattered about. She had not quite finished dressing, for she had but one shoe on,—the other was on the table near her hand,—her veil was but half arranged, her watch and chain were not put on, and some lace for her bosom lay with those trinkets, and with her handkerchief, and gloves, and some flowers, and a Prayer-Book all confusedly heaped about the looking-glass.

(continued on next page)

The first sentence of the excerpt, "*This was very uncomfortable, and I was half afraid,*" is a _____ sentence.
- ○ simple
- ○ compound
- ○ complex

Which of these words from the excerpt has a prefix that means "not"?
- ○ entered
- ○ arranged
- ○ unknown
- ○ materials

Which of these words from the excerpt has a suffix that means "most"?
- ○ dependent
- ○ dressing
- ○ confusedly
- ○ strangest

Which word describes the room in which the narrator finds himself in this scene?
- ○ comfortable
- ○ chaotic
- ○ tidy
- ○ dark

The woman in the scene appears to be...
- ○ rich
- ○ dirty
- ○ mute
- ○ young

Reread the excerpt from Charles Dickens' *Great Expectations* in lesson 145 and then answer the questions.

Based on the description given, it would seem the woman in this scene was a...
- ○ bride
- ○ fashion designer
- ○ beggar
- ○ we don't know

What does the narrator imply was his biggest clue that the prominent table in the room was *"a fine lady's dressing-table"*?
- ○ the gilded looking-glass
- ○ that it was a draped table
- ○ the fine lady sitting at it
- ○ the bright jewels

Which of these best portrays how the woman is likely feeling, given the described scene?
- ○ happy
- ○ energized
- ○ organized
- ○ sad

The narrator describes himself as...
- ○ uncomfortable
- ○ confident
- ○ timid
- ○ young

The narrator describes the woman as...
- ○ put together
- ○ boisterous
- ○ strange
- ○ messy

Reread the excerpt from Charles Dickens' *Great Expectations* in lesson 145 and then answer the questions.

All of the sentences in this excerpt are which type of sentence?
- ○ declarative
- ○ interrogative
- ○ exclamatory
- ○ imperative

Why did the woman only have one shoe on?
- ○ she hadn't put the other on yet (or had taken it off already)
- ○ she couldn't find the other shoe
- ○ she only had one leg
- ○ we don't know

Reread this line from the first paragraph: *This was very <u>uncomfortable</u>, and I was half afraid.* In which of these words does the suffix –able mean the same as it does in the word *uncomfortable*?
- ○ table
- ○ cable
- ○ doable
- ○ fable

A majority of this excerpt is which part of a story?
- ○ character development
- ○ a description of setting
- ○ plot
- ○ climax

What explanation of the scene would make sense given the information we have?
- ○ there was an earthquake
- ○ the woman's fiancé left her at the altar
- ○ the narrator was a robber
- ○ the electricity was out

Use this excerpt from Charles Dickens' *Oliver Twist* to answer the questions in lessons148-150.

Boys have generally excellent appetites. Oliver Twist and his companions suffered the tortures of slow starvation for three months: at last they got so voracious and wild with hunger, that one boy, who was tall for his age, and hadn't been used to that sort of thing (for his father had kept a small cook-shop), hinted darkly to his companions, that unless he had another basin of gruel per diem, he was afraid he might some night happen to eat the boy who slept next him, who happened to be a weakly youth of tender age. He had a wild, hungry eye; and they implicitly believed him. A council was held; lots were cast who should walk up to the master after supper that evening, and ask for more; and it fell to Oliver Twist.

The evening arrived; the boys took their places. The master, in his cook's uniform, stationed himself at the copper; his pauper assistants ranged themselves behind him; the gruel was served out; and a long grace was said over the short commons. The gruel disappeared; the boys whispered each other, and winked at Oliver; while his next neighbors nudged him. Child as he was, he was desperate with hunger, and reckless with misery. He rose from the table; and advancing to the master, basin and spoon in hand, said: somewhat alarmed at his own temerity:

"Please, sir, I want some more."

The master was a fat, healthy man; but he turned very pale. He gazed in stupefied astonishment on the small rebel for some seconds, and then clung for support to the copper. The assistants were paralysed with wonder; the boys with fear.

"What!" said the master at length, in a faint voice.

"Please, sir," replied Oliver, "I want some more."

The master aimed a blow at Oliver's head with the ladle; pinioned him in his arm; and shrieked aloud for the beadle.

(continued on next page)

The likely setting for this story, based on this passage, is...
- ○ an orphanage
- ○ a hospital
- ○ a police station
- ○ a library

What is the problem the boys are facing in this excerpt?
- ○ they're overworked
- ○ they're tired
- ○ they're hungry
- ○ they don't like the master

Which of these words from the excerpt has a suffix that means "full of"?
- ○ generally
- ○ voracious
- ○ companions
- ○ reckless

Read this part of a sentence from the excerpt: ...*the boy who slept next him, who happened to be a* <u>weakly</u> *youth of tender age.* The word *weakly* here is being used as a(n)...
- ○ noun
- ○ verb
- ○ adjective
- ○ adverb

The master was _____ Oliver's request.
- ○ pleased with
- ○ understanding of
- ○ depressed because of
- ○ furious about

Reread the excerpt from Charles Dickens' *Oliver Twist* in lesson 148 and then answer these questions.

Reread this partial sentence from the excerpt: *He rose from the table; and advancing to the master, basin and spoon in hand, said: somewhat alarmed at his own* <u>temerity</u>: *"Please, sir, I want some more."* Based on the context, a good synonym for *temerity* would be...

- ○ timidity
- ○ boldness
- ○ stupidity
- ○ friendliness

Does it seem that the assistants had ever heard an orphan ask for seconds?

- ○ yes
- ○ no

In this excerpt, what is *gruel*?

- ○ food
- ○ work
- ○ exhaustion
- ○ anger

Which of these words from the excerpt is a compound word?

- ○ hunger
- ○ pinioned
- ○ desperate
- ○ somewhat

True or false: Oliver came empty-handed for seconds.

- ○ true
- ○ false

Lesson 150: Reading Comprehension Language Arts 7

Reread the excerpt from Charles Dickens' *Oliver Twist* in lesson 148 and then answer these questions.

Which of these words from the excerpt has a suffix that means "characterized by"?
- ○ stupefied
- ○ paralysed
- ○ healthy
- ○ reckless

The excerpt explicitly states that the master was...
- ○ mean
- ○ fat
- ○ angry
- ○ hungry

What conflict is the main catalyst for the climax of this excerpt?
- ○ the boys are hungry
- ○ the master is mean

Read this sentence from the first paragraph: *Boys have generally excellent appetites.* – in which of these words does the suffix –ent mean the same as it does in the word *excellent*?
- ○ accent
- ○ percent
- ○ agent
- ○ absorbent

Did Oliver get his seconds?
- ○ yes
- ○ no

Lesson 151: Spellcheck

This paragraph contains five misspelled words. Can you figure out what they are and spell them correctly on the lines?

       Many scientists believe the world to be millions, if not billions, of years old. Various scientific publications repetedly state this as fact. However, there are a growing number of scientists who now believe the earth to be much younger than previously thought. Several dating methods have been proven to be inaccurate. Sometimes in science, the best we can do is speculait. Our speculations can coincied with available data, but no one can guarantie that their way is right. Altho some parts of our physical universe can be proven, many continue to be a mystery.

_____   _____

_____   _____

_____

Lesson 152: Metaphors • Genre

A metaphor is where one thing is said to be another. Examples from *The King Will Make A Way*:

- She was always at work, an ant in an apron. (ch. 1)
- The sun was a brilliant gold medallion adorning the sky. (ch. 5)
- Outside the storm was a rampaging drunk, toppling everything within its reach… (ch. 5)
- (The character is looking at a tree): Her eyes opened and stared up at the wooden ladder. She wondered what she could see if she climbed limb by limb up the rungs to its top. (ch. 14)
- A line formed, an ever shifting centipede, a hundred legs taking little steps forward… (ch. 27)

Make some of your own metaphors. Finish these sentences. Example: Summer is a new toy fresh out of the box. Why is summer like a new toy fresh out of the box? It's something new and exciting. It's a time we break from routine and do something different. Don't just use a word or two, be creative!

Winter is _____

_____

Ice cream is _____

_____

My family is _____

_____

*Remember, a metaphor is saying one thing is something else. DO NOT use like or as. ("As sly as a fox" or "happy like a song bird" are examples of similes, not metaphors.)

(continued on next page)

Lesson 152: Metaphors • Genre

Book genre simply means what type of book. Biography is a genre of nonfiction book that tells the story of a person's life. Other types of nonfiction book genres include reference, how-to, historic, scientific, sports, as well as many others.

Make a list of fiction genres you can think of: humor, western, _____

_____

_____

_____

Although not in its purest form, *The King Will Make a Way* is a type of allegory – one big metaphor. A metaphor is where one thing is said to be another. Some famous allegories are *Pilgrim's Progress* and *Animal Farm*. In *The King Will Make a Way* there is a King. He represents Jesus. The whole story you read in the book actually represents something else. As you read (if you're reading it), be mindful of the clues to show you what different things represent and what the story as a whole is about.

Choose a genre for your novel. Use the space below to write down any notes you'd like that pertain to your novel's genre.

_____

_____

_____

_____

As a reminder, a **simple sentence** is simple – just one subject and predicate combination. *This is an example of a simple sentence.*

A **compound sentence** takes two simple sentences and compounds them, squashes them together using something like—"and", "or", "but"—in the middle to connect them. *This is an example of a compound sentence, and I have made it with two simple sentences joined together into one.*

A **complex sentence** takes a simple sentence and adds another subject and predicate in a way that they don't form another sentence on their own. *This is an example of a complex sentence because I have added a second subject and verb in a way that can't stand on its own.*

Identify these sentence types (from ch. 3 of *The King Will Make a Way*). The answers are simple, compound, or complex.

He crouched and examined mushrooms, pine cones, rocks and beetles.

_____

Gabe kept up the maneuvers until the guard was safely settled back in his guard box, comfortably seated on his stool.

_____

The toad hopped off just beyond him, and the natural impulse of a ten-year-old boy to try and catch it overpowered him.

_____

He looked up and his heart melted.

_____

Unthinking, he flung himself at the King's feet.

_____

Even though the hill was just a few stone throws away from the inn, he felt like a pioneer—adventurous and alone.

_____

(continued on next page)

Fill out this form for your protagonist. Some may not apply. You can draw a picture of your main character in the box.

Name _____ Age _____

Job _____ Hair _____

Clothes _____ Home _____

Family _____. Music _____

Hobbies _____

Sports _____ Food _____

Favorite things _____

Things (s)he can't stand_____

Does for fun _____

Bad habits _____

Fears _____

Quirks _____

Catchphrase _____

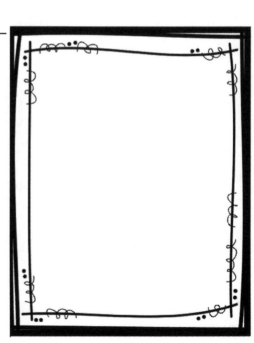

(continued on next page)

Lesson 153: Sentence Structure • Characters Language Arts 7

Fill out this form for your antagonist. Some may not apply. You can draw a picture of your villain in the box.

Name _____   Age _____

Job _____   Hair _____

Clothes _____   Home _____

Family _____   Music _____

Hobbies_____

Sports _____   Food _____

Favorite things _____

Things (s)he can't stand_____

Does for fun _____

Bad habits _____

Fears _____

Quirks _____

Catchphrase _____

Lesson 154: Conflict

Use this page to brainstorm what the conflict in your story will be.

What will set off your story? _____

_____

_____

_____

What is the big question in your book? _____

_____

_____

_____

What is the answer going to be? _____

_____

_____

_____

Lesson 155: Sidekicks • Descriptive Writing   Language Arts 7

Fill out this form for your protagonist's sidekick. Some may not apply. You can draw a picture of your sidekick in the box.

Name _____   Age _____

Job _____   Hair _____

Clothes _____   Home _____

Family _____   Music _____

Hobbies _____

Sports _____   Food _____

Favorite things _____

Things (s)he can't stand _____

Does for fun _____

Bad habits _____

Fears _____

Quirks _____

Catchphrase _____

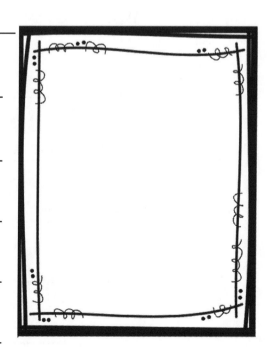

(continued on next page)

Fill out this form for your antagonist's sidekick. Some may not apply. You can draw a picture of your sidekick in the box.

Name _____   Age _____

Job _____   Hair _____

Clothes _____   Home _____

Family _____   Music _____

Hobbies _____

Sports _____   Food _____

Favorite things _____

Things (s)he can't stand_____

Does for fun _____

Bad habits _____

Fears _____

Quirks _____

Catchphrase _____

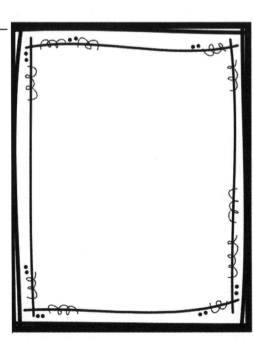

(continued on next page)

Pick a place everyone in your family knows and describe it. Use all five senses. Don't use names or in any way tell them the answer in the description. See if they can figure out what you described.

_____

_____

_____

_____

_____

_____

Now write a description of a person everyone in your family knows. Again, don't give the answer, but describe the answer.

_____

_____

_____

_____

_____

_____

What is the overall setting of your book going to be? Fill in this page about your setting. You can use the bottom to sketch a picture of it if you'd like.

Time: _____

Description:_____

_____

_____

_____

(continued on next page)

As a reminder, there are four types of sentences: declarative, interrogative, exclamatory, and imperative.

Declarative sentences make statements. *Today is my birthday.*

Interrogative sentences ask questions. *Is today your birthday?*

Exclamatory sentences exclaim. *Today is my birthday!*

Imperative sentences command. *Today's your birthday, so celebrate!*

Identify the sentence types of the sentences from chapter 5 of *The King Will Make a Way*.

He sat up straighter.   _____

When is it coming?   _____

Relax.   _____

What are you saying?   _____

Father was worried.   _____

Yes, sir!   _____

Get inside and stay there!   _____

This is going to be a bad storm!   _____

Tabitha shrieked.   _____

Remember the old village song?   _____

Describe some of the minor settings in your book and how they will be used.

_____

_____

_____

_____

_____

_____

_____

_____

_____

_____

(continued on next page)

Lesson 157: Setting • Parallel Sentences

Language Arts 7

One way to show time passing quickly in your story is to use parallel sentences — sentences that have the same structure. Here's an example from chapter 6 of *The King Will Make a Way*: "The spring rain showered. The summer heat scorched. The fall apples ripened. The lake froze. The flowers bloomed. The corn was knee high. The harvest was gathered. Eggs hatched; bees buzzed; leaves tumbled."

Choose a time of year and write parallel sentences that tell your audience when you are talking about. It doesn't have to be a season. It could be Christmas time for example. Don't say it outright. Describe the time of year. Try to use all five senses!

_____

_____

_____

_____

_____

_____

_____

_____

Make a list of five objects you can put into your story. Then make a list of complications that could arise for your protagonist and antagonist. If you get stuck while writing, you can look at the lists to help spark an idea.

Objects:

_____

_____

_____

_____

Complications:

_____

_____

_____

_____

Lesson 159: Plot Chart

Fill out this plot chart for your novel.

Title:_____

Main Character	Goal/Problem to Solve	Villain/Obstacle	Supporting Characters

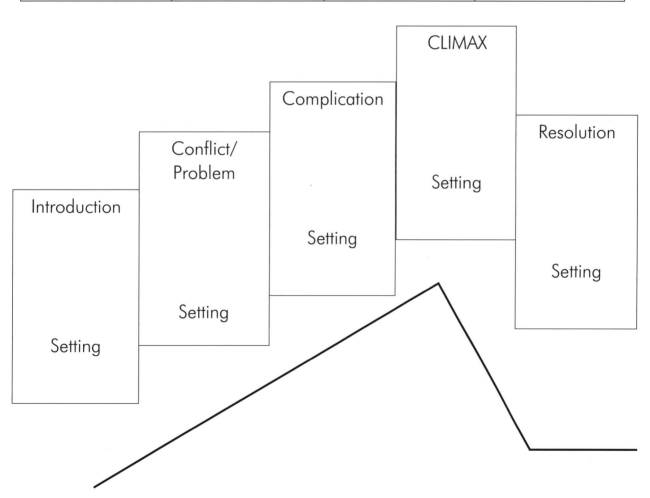

Make a list of chapter titles for your novel.

_____

_____

_____

_____

_____

_____

_____

_____

_____

_____

Irony is when something is the opposite of what you would expect. A fire station catching on fire would be ironic. A murderer getting the death sentence as a punishment is ironic.

An **oxymoron** is when two contradictory terms are used together. Some examples are *jumbo shrimp, act naturally, only choice, alone together.*

Can you think of other examples of irony or oxymorons?

_____

_____

_____

_____

_____

_____

_____

_____

_____

Lesson 163: Dialogue

Properly punctuate the dialogue at the top of the page. Then use the lines at the bottom of the page to write a dialogue of your own.

Come here he said

She got up and crossed the room What is it

A geode.

She asked again And that is what exactly

He brought out a hammer Watch and see.

_____

_____

_____

_____

_____

_____

Lesson 164: Uncommon Punctuation

Add the missing punctuation to this sentence. Be sure to include any uncommon punctuation (semicolon, colon, dash).

I had too much on my mind so I got out of bed to make myself a list of what I needed to do call mom Jenny and the plumber bake the cookies take pictures of the kids and update the blog just so I could get some sleep

Write a sentence or a paragraph that uses a semicolon, a colon, and a dash.

_____

_____

_____

_____

_____

_____

_____

Find examples of metaphor in a book you are currently reading and write them on the lines. Come up with your own examples of metaphors if you'd like. Can you incorporate some metaphor into your novel?

Here's an example from *The King Will Make a Way*:

> *"He knew of their meetings and their disloyalty, but they were a bunch of weaklings: women, children and old men, only a few straggly others joined them. There were the rooks, his guards; the queen, his devoted servants whom he could bid come to his side at a moment's notice; and he, of course, was the king. That left the knights, those horses that fancied themselves special—the only pieces on a chess board allowed to jump over another."*

_____

_____

_____

_____

_____

_____

_____

_____

Lesson 166: Anthropomorphism

Language Arts 7

Anthropomorphism is a literary device where something non-human becomes humanlike in form and/or behavior. Read this sentence from chapter 15 of *The King Will Make a Way*:

Despair circled Gabe like a vulture, taunting, laughing. "He's dead. He's dead. They're all dead. Lifeless bodies left for the birds. You might as well join them. Vulpine will be after you next."

What nonliving thing is taking on human attributes? _____

What human qualities did it have? _____

_____

Now you try it. Look at the pen or pencil in your hand. Make it come alive. What is it thinking as you are holding it, writing with it? What would it say when you are chewing on it, tapping it? Give it a personality and write a little story with the pen or pencil as the main character. Give his point of view on the world.

_____

_____

_____

_____

_____

_____

_____

Lesson 167: Lie vs. Lay

In the present tense, lie is what you do to yourself, and lay is what you do to something else. Fill in these blanks with lie or lay:

I _____ on my bed to rest.

A chicken _____s an egg.

In the past tense, lie becomes lay, and lay becomes laid. Fill in these blanks with lie, lay, or laid:

I want to _____ down for a nap.

Last week I _____ out the pattern for the dress.

I need to _____ out the schedule for everyone to see.

He _____ there for hours yesterday.

See if you can figure out the correct word for each blank.

My cat is _____ in the light.
   ○ laying   ○ lying

She often _____ there.
   ○ lies   ○ lays

I _____ my toothbrush on the sink.
   ○ lay   ○ laid

The US _____ to the north of Mexico.
   ○ lies   ○ lays

Lesson 171: Personification

Personification is when something inanimate is described as if it were animate. Here are some weather examples:

A soft rain tiptoed across the lawn.
The snow threw a white blanket over the lawn.
The sun smiled down on the lawn.

Choose a type of weather (sunny, windy, rainy, cloudy...) and describe what is happening using personification. Use the examples above to help you. Then do it again with another type of weather.

_____

_____

_____

_____

_____

_____

_____

_____

_____

Lesson 177: Alliteration

Alliteration is the repeating of the initial consonant sound in a series of words. Familiar examples might include Mickey Mouse, Donald Duck, or Peter Piper picked a peck of pickled peppers.

Write ten alliterations. Write at least two with 3 words and two with 4 words. See how many words you can string together in your longest one.

1._____

2._____

3._____

4._____

5._____

6._____

7._____

8._____

9._____

10._____

Lesson 178: Onomatopoeia

Language Arts 7

Onomatopoeia is when the name of the sound is associated with the sound. Words that make the sound they describe would be another way to say it. Here are some examples: bam, clatter, clap, mumble, pop, swoosh, rattle, thud, shuffle, whisper, buzz.

Write a short story about a morning in your home, from the time you get up until breakfast. Use as many sound words as you can in your story.

_____

_____

_____

_____

_____

_____

_____

_____

_____

_____

_____

Congratulations!

You have finished Language Arts 7!

The Easy Peasy All-in-One Homeschool is a free, complete online homeschool curriculum. There are 180 days of ready-to-go assignments for every level and every subject. It's created for your children to work as independently as you want them to. Preschool through high school is available as well as courses ranging from English, math, science, and history to art, music, computer, thinking, physical education, and health. A daily Bible lesson is offered as well. The mission of Easy Peasy is to enable those to homeschool who otherwise thought they couldn't.

The Genesis Curriculum takes the Bible and turns it into lessons for your homeschool. Daily lessons include Bible reading, memory verse, spelling, handwriting, vocabulary, grammar, Biblical language, science, social studies, writing, and thinking through discussion questions.

The Genesis Curriculum uses a complete book of the Bible for one full year. The curriculum is being made using both Old and New Testament books. Find us online at genesiscurriculum.com to read about the latest developments in this expanding curriculum.

Made in the USA
Coppell, TX
08 May 2024

32176521R00094